A MORAL STANCE

It's a story that
had to be told—

Cary Nelson

A MORAL STANCE

'51 UNIVERSITY OF SAN FRANCISCO FIGHT AGAINST DISCRIMINATION

GARY (DOC) NELSON

Waterside Publishing

Printed in the United States of America

First Printing, 2019

ISBN-13: 978-1-941768-42-6 print edition
ISBN-13: 978-1-941768-43-3 ebook edition

Waterside Productions
2055 Oxford Ave
Cardiff, CA 92007
www.waterside.com

THE LEGEND

January 2, 2007 – Fiesta Bowl

It was dark in the tunnel. Through the opening some fifteen yards from where the group huddled, the sun shone brightly on the field where West Virginia drove toward the Oklahoma Sooners' goal line. The men introduced themselves to the pretty young women who were to be their escorts onto the field at halftime. There was one escort for each of the men. An organizer stood in front of them, his back to the bright light that was the field. After a PA introduction, each man was to walk single file with one of the escorts at his side to the fifty-yard line. The stadium PA would then tell their story. They would turn 360 degrees for the crowd's benefit, then walk off single file. There were only two minutes left in the second quarter, so it would be soon.

One of the men would not walk to center field. Burl Toler was unable to walk and was in a wheelchair. The organizer had supplied a volunteer who would roll Burl out. As the word was passed to the organizer, he announced, "Here we go!" and waved the first member of the '51 team out into the sunlight. Bill Henneberry moved out onto the track and stopped, turning backward and offering his hand to the man following. He moved slowly to his left and those following, no longer in single file, grasped the hands of the adjacent players. As the end of the line came out of the tunnel, the end man moved to the right and joined with Henneberry, forming a circle. As a circle, they moved out onto the field.

At first the director tried to correct them, but then gave up as a great roar came from the 55,000 spectators. Usually as soon as the half-time whistle blows, the fans head for the concession stands or the bathrooms. Having heard the announcement of the 1951 USF Dons team, however, most had not moved from their seats; the crowd seemed aware that they were witnessing greatness. Together the players moved hand in hand to the center of the field. Gino Marchetti waved the volunteer away and rolled Burl into the circle himself next to Ollie Matson, then stepped between them and joined the circle, grasping their hands on either side. One by one they were introduced over the PA. As their names were called, the men did not break the circle; they raised their hands, still holding the two hands next to them. The young escorts stood behind each player.

After all the names had been called, the director motioned the players to move off the field, but the crowd wouldn't let them go. Each time they moved, the ovation became louder. As if on cue, the men reached back to the young women and brought them into the circle as well. It was as they had played, connected as one: a family of different individuals, from different places, with different upbringings, but all acting with a common purpose.

The second half of the Fiesta Bowl was delayed by almost eight minutes as the crowd continued to cheer. As the young women walked off the field, hand in hand with the players, their faces were streaked with tears.

CHAPTER ONE

San Francisco in the late nineteen-forties and early fifties was a city undergoing change. Before World War II, it had been a city of around five hundred thousand, divided into defined neighborhoods as much by ethnicity as by the city's topography. There was North Beach (Italian), Chinatown, South of Market (Irish), and Latino neighborhoods south of them. There was even Little Sweden, adjacent to the campus of the University of San Francisco, recognizable by the Norse gingerbread on the facings of the Victorian houses sitting on streets named Fell, Hayes, and Grove.

During and immediately after the war, the population of the city increased by over two hundred thousand people, beginning a breakdown of the rigid boundaries of the established neighborhoods. People who came to the west coast with the armed services during the war tended to stay. Those who passed through on their way to the Pacific theater returned and settled. Families had children, and those children born during the Depression— living through the war fighting Germany and Japan, enduring those years with blackout shades, Spam, and the threat of Japanese submarines off the Golden Gate—looked to college.

The Korean war was an inevitable conflict given what was left of the existing power structures at the end of the previous hostilities. Korea had a civil war, the North supported by the new Communist China and the South by the United States. When

1

it was finally settled, there were two Koreas, the dividing line the 38th parallel, which by coincidence ran directly through San Francisco. At the University of San Francisco, the war was felt in several ways. The campus was filled with World War II Quonset huts that were used for offices, classrooms, and dormitories. These were kept well beyond their normal usefulness. The end of World War II also brought about the signing in 1944 of the Servicemen's Readjustment Act, known as the G. I. Bill. This legislation provided a range of benefits for the returning servicemen, including free tuition to colleges. It greatly skewed the age range of incoming college students, particularly male students.

At the time the Korean War began, the university had an all-male student body. College did not earn you a deferral from the military draft as it would in future times. As a result, USF's enrollment began to decline and would continue to do so until the end of the war in Korea. The Jesuits who had founded the University of San Francisco a hundred years before felt the strain of the shrinking student body on their private institution, prayed for the end of the conflict, and implemented several cost-cutting measures. Like most Jesuit colleges in the United States, USF had as its major focuses scholarship, community involvement, and athletics. In 1951, athletics meant basketball and football, and both contribute mightily to this story, because that year, USF had a football team that went undefeated and untied. The team's publicity manager was a graduate student named Pete Rozelle.

CHAPTER TWO

1986
New York City

A fair-haired man with an unremarkable face, wearing a dark blue suit, stepped into an elevator at 410 Park Avenue. He automatically pushed the button for the fiftieth floor, moving aside for three other passengers who entered after him. The lift swayed side to side as it rose, stopping twice to discharge two of the three passengers before stopping at his chosen floor. The third passenger, a striking woman wearing a tailored skirt and jacket, started for the door at the same time as he did, provoking a slightly embarrassed pardon from the man before he followed her out into the carpeted hallway. He watched her walk down the hallway to the right before turning left himself and entering an impressive oak-paneled office, the headquarters of the National Football League.

Getting a smile and a nod from Rozelle's gatekeeper and executive secretary, Thelma Elkjer, who occupied an entry office as opulent and much more functional than Rozelle's, the man, Jim Kensil, continued straight into the private office of Pete Rozelle. The commissioner had a phone to his ear and a pen in his hand. He looked up and slanted his head toward the couch that took up part of the east wall of his corner office.

The office was luxurious, the skyline of New York high-lighted in the floor-to-ceiling window behind Rozelle's desk. The light streaming in from the late-morning sun softened the effect of the rich leather furniture and deep wood paneling. If the light did not give the room a feeling of powerful informality, Rozelle certainly did. Every so often he would put down his pen and pick up a cigarette from a pack next to the nearly full ashtray. With smoke circling above him, he took up his pen again to scribble a few more notes, only stopping to sip from a crystal glass full of amber fluid. He hung up the phone, only to have it ring again almost immediately. When he picked up the receiver again, he was animated, smiling broadly for a second into the mouthpiece as if his cheerful expression could be transmitted over the wire. As fast as his smile appeared, it disappeared, transforming as he spoke into a thin-lipped scowl.

"Sid, I don't want to hear it."

Sid Gillman was on the line, giving his support to Al Davis's recommendation to put an NFL franchise into Las Vegas. Kensil knew that Rozelle was strenuously against it, and from the sound of the phone call he was not happy that Gillman was taking Davis's side. Rozelle was not against it only because of it being Davis's motion, although that would have been enough; he was concerned about the issue of gambling that was associated with the Nevada town.

"Look, Sid, I suspended Paul Hornung and Alex Karras in 1963 for placing bets with hoodlums," Kensil heard Rozelle say.

It had not been the first test of Rozelle's strength as com-missioner—revenue sharing and moving the main offices to New York had the claim to that—but it was his first crisis. Hornung had accepted the year-long suspension with grace and class, apologizing to his coach, Vince Lombardi, and even to Rozelle in a letter when his suspension was over. But Karras just got angry, very angry, when Rozelle called him with the news of his indefinite suspension. There was solid proof that Karras had bet on Detroit Lions games and facilitated five of his teammates in doing the same. He also owned a piece of a bar with known criminals Jimmy and John Butsicaris. Nevertheless, Karras claimed he was not guilty and hired an attorney. The suspension stuck. Kensil knew that if it hadn't been for the high profiles of Hornung and Karras, the Detroit organization's involvement would have been the bigger story.

"You know that Detroit's management was my biggest worry. They ignored a police report telling them about multiple incidents of contact between mob members and their players. They even allowed these members on the sidelines and on the team bus, for Christ's sake. What do our fans think would happen if we put a team in Sin City? The rumors alone would kill us."

Rozelle's genius had shown itself in the press conference he held immediately after the phone calls of their suspensions to Hornung and Karras. He emphasized the Hornung and Karras suspensions and that there had been no point shaving, as all bets had been made on their own teams winning. He mentioned that others might be fined as the investigation concluded, but as he had hoped, little was made of the Lions management and the other players who were involved. Eventually the Detroit Lions ownership was fined $4,000 due to not having acted on the police report, and the players who were not suspended were fined $1,000 or more for placing their bets. Rozelle knew the NFL must be above reproach. If there was even a hint of funny business, it would lose its credibility and with it the fans.

"Sid, Las Vegas is out of the question. The NFL has to maintain a crystal clean image when it comes to gambling," said Rozelle. He listened for a few more seconds, then said he looked forward to having dinner with Gillman later that week and hung up.

Rozelle turned to the man on the couch. "Damned Davis. Must the man oppose me on every issue, even one as obvious as this one?"

Jim Kensil had been one of Rozelle's first hires. Kensil had been in the Associated Press's sports department. Years before, Rozelle had agreed to an interview about how he planned to expand the NFL's content on television. Rozelle neatly reversed the roles in the interview, getting the newspaper man's opinion on a range of topics, including the television package, then offered him a job as his assistant.

"The man wants your job, boss. He was soundly voted down in the merger, and he took it personally. Every one of your moves has been exactly what professional football needed at the time."

Rozelle shook his head and smiled. He knew exactly how each of his moves had contributed to the popularity of the National Football League. When he had taken over and moved the headquarters to New York, they'd had seven staff members. By 1986 the organization employed over nine hundred. He had started with twelve teams in 1960, with only four of them making money. Barely half the seats were filled. Now there were twenty-eight teams, all making money and lots of it. The Super Bowl out west at Stanford the previous January had more people watching on television than any live event in history. Granted, it was a great match-up—east and west with the 49ers and Montana beating Miami and Marino. Rozelle had even recruited Ronald Reagan, the President of the United States, to do the coin toss.

"Revenue sharing was the key," said Rozelle. "All the rest fell into place because of that."

Kensil knew that it had been a major win for Rozelle to get the owners to agree to revenue sharing. With that in his hand he had lobbied Congress to give the league an exemption from anti-trust laws, which allowed the original twelve owners to place their gates and broadcast rights into the NFL pot. Congress passed the legislation and President Jack Kennedy signed it. As soon as the smaller markets became competitive, people started taking notice, but the gambling thing was almost as important. Rozelle was not naïve. He knew that betting on games added to the interest, especially among fans who watched the TV coverage. This was especially true now that Kensil had most of the games on TV. Rozelle had said more than once, though, that everything he had built could be lost if there was a hint that the games could be fixed. He knew the NFL must remain clear of any hint of involvement in anything underhanded, and that particularly meant gambling. It meant the league staff, the owners, the game officials, and especially the players.

Of all the owners, Davis, the part owner and general manager of the Oakland Raiders, gave Rozelle the most trouble. When Rozelle had incorporated the rival American Football League into the NFL, Davis had lost the battle to unseat Rozelle as commissioner. If Rozelle said the sky was blue, Davis would say it was green. He was an attorney and was constantly bringing suits against the league when he didn't get his way.

"Gillman, of all the owners, should know better, or at least have the smarts to understand the objections." Rozelle rose and walked to the bar, pouring himself another glass of scotch and one for Kensil as well. He handed off the tumbler and rolled his chair from behind the desk until it faced the couch.

Rozelle considered drinking an integral part of the commissioner's job. He swirled his drink, watching as it coated the inside of the tumbler before slowly returning to the inch of amber liquid in the bottom. He brought his nose to the rim of the glass and took a deep breath, exhaling slowly, with pleasure. "I learned about single malt scotch at the University of San Francisco in '51. Most of the coaches I dealt with there drank it. It was easy to catch the habit. Before then I just drank beer, usually not very good beer. The school had a bar on campus if you can believe it, not just for the faculty and staff, but for the students as well; the coaching staff often went there after practice."

Rozelle looked at the amber liquid in his glass. Every time he had a conversation on a moral issue like the one with Gillman, even if it had the bottom line as the crux of the issue, he thought back to his time at USF. He remembered a sign above the bar written in raised wooden letters above a background of green: *Honor. Change the world from here.* Honor, doing what's right, and scotch whiskey—those are pretty good life lessons, and that was much of what he remembered from USF.

In 1950, Rozelle was already a man. He had graduated from high school, been to two years of college, and spent three years on a fuel ship in the Pacific, but it was those years at USF, finishing his studies and working with the football team, that had shown him how to live his life. It had been over thirty years ago, but to Rozelle it seemed like yesterday. Sometimes, on days when he had to deal with all the crap coming out of the owners' meetings, he would think about that '51 season at USF and how the players had all stood together. It was one of the most exciting years of his life, and in private he often said that it was the greatest team he had ever seen … in college and maybe even in the pros.

In 1950, USF was a little jewel of a college in San Francisco. It had just over a thousand students, all male. It was run by Father William Dunne, a Jesuit, a great organizer with a firm grasp of the bottom line. Rozelle said in later years that Dunne could have run the NFL. Just after graduating, Rozelle had gone to the president's office looking for a job in the athletic department. As a student the year before, he had worked for free for Pete Newell, the basketball coach. He had Newell's recommendation in his hand, growing damp from nervous sweat.

Rozelle was fifteen minutes early, but he was ushered into the president's office. Father Dunne was talking to another Jesuit, Father Feeley, who Pete knew was a sports junkie, particularly when it came to football. Pete had taken a course from him the previous year and received an A. Seeing him gave Rozelle a small lift of confidence.

"Congratulations on your graduation, Pete," said Father Feeley, trying to set Rozelle at ease, something that Father Dunne was not likely to do.

In a monotone, Dunne asked what he could do for Pete.

"I would really like to stay at USF and take a grad program in business. I heard there was going to be a position for sports publicity director opening up and I wanted to apply."

"Pete has done a good job on the school paper for the last two years," interjected Feeley, "and Coach Newell thinks highly of the work he did for the basketball team last year."

Father Dunne explained that it would be a new position and Pete would have to work to define it with all the coaches, not just Coach Newell. Tuition for the grad program would of course be waived. Pete couldn't believe what he was hearing. Later he learned that the position had already been set up and both Feeley and Coach Newell had greased the skids. At the time, though, he was clueless and just asked if he would get paid. Dunne said yes, though probably not quite enough to meet his needs. Rozelle accepted so quickly he almost interrupted Dunne's last sentence. And so it began.

CHAPTER THREE

Rozelle, now well into his third scotch, leaned back in his chair and checked the clock. It was just after four. He started arranging the papers on his desk, putting some in drawers and others in a file holder to his right, and then he looked back at Jim Kensil, who had come back into the office after attending to work in his own. Kensil knew about his boss's start in football with the USF team.

Rozelle paused as he closed the file drawer, turning his chair as Kensil sat back down on the couch. "Do you know," he said, as if there had been no time lost since the man had left, "how rare it was to have all that talent gathered together in one little school? I mean, they had a few excellent recruits from all over the country. Sachs from Pasadena, Dwyer from Chicago, Madden from Omaha, Sakowski from Pennsylvania coal country, Thomas from Wisconsin, but the very best, the ones who went on to greatness, the ones we saw in the NFL, were local kids from San Francisco. The freshman coach and the USF team trainer had gone out and dug up every one of them, and some of them took a lot of digging. You know, Jim, I've told this story a dozen times, but never the whole story. Would you mind if I taped it?"

Getting a nod from Kensil, Rozelle turned to the bookcase and threaded a new tape reel into a professional Ampex tape recorder, flipping a toggle switch and scooting his chair back to his desk, where he pulled a microphone close to him. Kensil settled back against the couch cushions. He didn't want to miss a word of the story that was about to unfold.

AUGUST 13, 1950

Rozelle was there for the first meeting prior to the '50 season, mainly out of curiosity. He was still spending most of his time with the basketball team, but he had helped promote the soccer team with some success during the summer, so he was asked to lend support to the football staff; its season was in the fall, and basketball wouldn't be underway until winter and spring. The differences in the personalities of the athletes came as a revelation to Rozelle when he met them, and he wondered how the group would ever become a team.

It was the second Sunday in August 1950 when the team gathered to leave for their summer training camp. Rozelle was watching from the waiting room outside the President's office as a green-and-white city bus pulled away from the curb on Fulton Street, revealing a giant of a man who, after looking to his left, jaywalked across the road and through the iron gate that led to a section of grass in front of the university's administration building. A small group of players had already congregated, having just arrived on the previous bus. Father Feeley was standing next to the new publicity director, giving Rozelle the names and backgrounds of the arriving players. He knew them all, maybe better than some of the coaches. Wearing suits and ties, waiting for the others to arrive, were Merrill Peacock, Ollie Matson, Vince Tringali, and Bill Henneberry, who looked diminutive standing next to the others.

As the young giant took the steps two by two, a smile spreading across a handsome face that looked like it had not yet seen a razor, he was greeted first by Henneberry and then by the others as "Geek." Bob St. Clair was an incoming sophomore, straight off the undefeated freshman team, explained Feeley. At 6'8 and

265 pounds, he towered over the others, even Peacock, who had entered school as a running back and was now St. Clair's counterpart as a pass-catching end. St. Clair slapped Peacock on the back and had started to say something when a car honked three times. All of them turned toward the street, where a 1948 Buick convertible was pulling up to the curb. There were three girls in the bright blue car with a good-looking young man driving.

The driver got out and kissed the girl next to him, who slid over to take the wheel; then he repeated the kiss with each of the backseat passengers before bounding up the stairs and through the wrought-iron gate, stopping halfway up to wave at the girls in the car as they pulled away. Ed Brown—starting his second year as quarterback, movie-star handsome with a reputation with the ladies to maintain—pulled out a comb and slid it smoothly through his black hair. He yelled, "Geek!" as he approached St. Clair, welcoming the big end to the varsity with a slap on the back.

Inside the administration building, six men watched with Rozelle as the group grew in number. Joe Kuharich, entering his second season as head football coach, looked at his watch, then back at the assembly growing outside the window. With him was Bud Kerr, his first assistant, who coached the linemen, James Ryan, the backfield coach, Brad Lynn, the freshman coach who was Kuharich's main recruiter, and Scrap Iron Young, the team's trainer. All three of the assistants were young, handsome men in contrast to the head coach. Kuharich was a fireplug of a man with a jaw that even at rest appeared hostile. It married perfectly with his eyes, dark and deep-set, flicking from player to player. If you had to draw from imagination what a football coach should look like, you would end up with a likeness of Kuharich. His physical appearance, his perpetual frown, and the way he held his body radiated authority. Only his voice did not fit the man. It was oddly high-pitched, disconcerting as it emanated from a neck in a 20-inch shirt collar.

Rozelle was definitely the outsider in the group. He had concentrated on basketball the previous year, and his taking upper-level classes had kept him from getting to know most of the undergraduate athletes—although it was hard to miss the basketball and football players around campus because of their sheer physical presence. If it wouldn't have made him look stupid, he would have taken notes on what Father Feeley was saying, especially when he described the junior college transfers Matson, Toler, and Marchetti. Rozelle understood that he would have to get to know all thirty-nine like brothers if he was to do the job justice. The coaches looked at the players from a different perspective, as if they were picking out pieces of meat from the butcher's display at the market just down the street.

Scrap Iron Young checked off thirty-one names, referring to a clipboard without looking at his boss. He knew Kuharich insisted that five minutes early was late for his meetings. There were seven left to arrive, and Scrap Iron was his watch dog.

As they waited, a small figure exited the church, jumping the six steps in one leap, and walked with a slightly bow-legged gait directly across the grass to where St. Clair was standing. At five-foot-seven and 150 pounds, Joe Scudero barely reached St. Clair's shoulder. As he approached, he pointed his finger at the big man and started jabbing it at his chest. Kuharich wondered if he was going to have trouble with those two, as they had been recruited as bitter rivals from high school.

In a pre-season staff meeting, Brad Lynn had told Kuharich that he'd kept the two apart on the freshman squad and never let them practice directly against each other. Most of it was that Scudero was such a tough kid. He would fight a gorilla if you gave the gorilla a bat. Kuharich had said to get the best local talent, and Scudero was the best running back on the team, after Matson. Scudero might want to, but Kuharich didn't see him hurting St. Clair. Their fierce rivalry was rooted in a conflict that had occurred during a game in high school; St. Clair had clothes-lined Scudero as he came through the line and knocked him out, closing his right eye for the rest of the game.

The budding confrontation was interrupted by the deep roar of a motorcycle. Wearing dark shades, Gino Marchetti cruised up Fulton Street on a Harley, an Army duffel bag strapped behind him. He was wearing a black leather jacket with a white T-shirt and engineer boots. He gunned the engine for effect before turning the bike off.

Lynn had recruited Gino Marchetti out of Modesto Junior College in the Central Valley, where Marchetti was taking advantage of the G.I. Bill. Lynn was actually looking to recruit his brother, but Gino proved to be the better athlete. He was rough, having played only one year of football, but his size and athleticism led to his recruitment. Marchetti had received no other offers, but even so, Lynn had felt lucky in getting him. For his part, Kuharich trusted Lynn's eye for talent but was not impressed with Marchetti's clothes or Harley Davidson wheels, thinking that he looked like a punk.

At five before the hour, Scrap Iron looked at his list and saw that only one name was not checked off: Dwyer. Then he noticed him standing next to Ralph Thomas.

Kuharich had Brad Lynn get the driver and bring the bus up in front of the school. Then he led the rest of the group out through the secretary's room, Father Feeley and Rozelle falling in at the end of the line. They left the building, starting across the lawn toward the loose assembly of players. The bus, having pulled up at the curb, was already packed with the coaches' bags and the uniforms and equipment the players would use in the pre-season camp. Rozelle hustled after Coach Kuharich with a stack of blank personal biographies in his hand that he wanted the players to fill out during the bus ride to the camp.

Kuharich stepped up in front of the group. All the players came to attention. His I'm-the-one-in-charge presence immediately discouraged any more grab-ass. His coaching staff lined up behind him.

"Good morning, men. I think you know Coach Kerr, Coach Ryan, and Scrap Iron."

Young did not look up from his clipboard. In truth, he was out of place in this group of coaches. He was older, educated, with a law degree from Notre Dame without looking like it. Upon first meeting him, Rozelle thought he held the job based on the fact that he was clearly a tough man. His face looked like it had been hit with a snow shovel, several times in fact. His nose wandered first to the right and then to the left, where it terminated in a flattened bulb. He was fiercely loyal to Kuharich, who sent Scrap Iron when he wanted to recruit from a tough area, like Pennsylvania coal country. The players who knew him loved him for his devotion to Kuharich, which they understood extended to them as well.

"I want you to meet Pete Rozelle. Pete is the new news director. You can talk to him freely. It's his job to make sure the papers spell your names right." He then told the team what was expected of them: that they had a chance to be better than the previous year. His philosophy was simply winning—in school, with teammates, and on the field of competition.

His voice rising, Kuharich said, "Winning will start with the camp, which this year will be held away from campus. Be prepared to produce, to give it your all, or get out. I'm not vacillating you."

The players tried to stifle their mirth at the coach's malapropism. The ones from the previous year were used to this idiosyncrasy in their coach and shook their heads warningly to the newbies when they began to comment. Then they picked up their bags and started moving to the bus.

Rozelle ran quickly around the players and positioned himself just below the bus steps. As the players moved by him, he handed each a mimeographed bio and a pencil. The coaches, followed by Scrap Iron, entered last and took the first two rows on either side of the aisle behind the driver. The players seemed to know that those seats were reserved for the coaching crew and the trainer. Scrap Iron used the vacant seat next to him to pile his medical bag and ever-present clipboard.

Rozelle climbed on and walked toward the back, noticing that Bill Henneberry, the player Kuharich had penciled in as backup quarterback and defensive back, had an empty seat next to him. He knew that Henneberry had just been elected class president. Three rows behind him, across the aisle, there was a second empty seat next to Gino Marchetti, but Marchetti's shoulders took up his own seat and half the one next to him.

CHAPTER FOUR

"I was still making my way down the aisle as the bus pulled away from the school," Rozelle said to Kensil, still his rapt listener. "I looked back at the church on the crest of the hill, the highest spot on Fulton Street. The University of San Francisco wasn't always located on the Hilltop, you know, but the church had been there since 1914. I'll admit I didn't care a whit about the school's history when I applied out of junior college—just its academic standing and the fact that I had met the basketball coach when USF played USC down south. Nor had I bothered to learn much about the school's past while I was an undergrad. But when I knew I was going to apply for a job, and do it in front of Father Dunne, it seemed like a good idea to study up."

What Rozelle learned was actually quite interesting, going back all the way to the California Gold Rush. The school had started as Saint Ignatius College in 1855, a hastily thrown together series of temporary wooden structures located in the dunes covering much of San Francisco's eastern land mass, now the city's financial district. A half-mile of sand separated it from the commercial areas clustered around the waterfront. San Francisco was then still in the throes of the Gold Rush of 1849. In a way, it was the Gold Rush that prompted the Jesuit Antonio Maraschi to start the first school of higher learning in the city. No one has ever accused the Jesuits of being on the low end of the intelligence scale. Maraschi saw a need and sought to fill it. Under his guidance, a permanent school and church were soon built on the south side of Market Street between Fourth and Fifth Street. A large three-story brick structure encompassed St. Ignatius Church and the attached St. Ignatius College. The "new school" opened in 1863, dwarfing the nearby buildings. Its main focus was the teaching of science, specifically chemical engineering, which fit perfectly with the city's need for assayers and mining engineers.

The new building attracted a series of world-renowned Jesuit scientists, especially mathematicians, chemists, and engineers. The classes were filled with students who helped meet the needs of the increasing number of mines, not only of gold but of copper and silver, which were being discovered seemingly every day. By the close of 1863, the college had 474 students.

You can't get far into the history of early San Francisco without discussing the effects of the earthquake of April 18, 1906. The quake was devastating, especially to brick structures, and the three-story church of St. Ignatius and St. Ignatius College were both made of brick. They were leveled, destroyed with all their contents. As bad as the quake was, the resulting fires from the severed gas lines were worse. Almost all the buildings east of Van Ness Avenue were destroyed. The blocks of houses all along Van Ness were dynamited, preventing the fire from leaping to the west and thus preserving some of the grand Victorian houses there, leaving Van Ness as a six-lane thoroughfare from Market Street to the south to the Bay in the north. Some 80% of the total property value of San Francisco was destroyed. As the city started to rebuild, land near the Bay waterfront became expensive. The Jesuits, seeing the trend, sold their original property and acquired much greater acreage three miles to the west on a hilltop adjacent to a cemetery, where they planned to build a new church.

St. Ignatius College occupied three temporary homes over the next twenty-one years until it was moved to its Hilltop location in 1927, next to the magnificent new St. Ignatius Church, which had preceded the school to the present site thirteen years earlier. Once the school's move was complete, the institution became known as the University of San Francisco.

Rozelle resumed his story. "The bus was jostling the players and coaches alike, stopping and starting and taking a sharp left turn onto Oak Street. I was still standing in the aisle, and I kept looking around at the players further back. I considered the empty seat next to Henneberry. I already knew Henneberry from a class we had taken together the year before. He was smart, and he was a choirboy. In some ways Bill might have been the perfect start for me, but I felt success in my role as publicity director depended on feeding the press interesting stories that would make popular heroes of the players and bring fans to the games to fill Kezar Stadium. Writing about a backup player who lived at home, had an older sister named Rose who was a nun, and whose idea of excitement was taking a new bus route wouldn't grab the sports writers' attention.

"As the season went on, I became friends with Bill and found that he really was a choirboy. He did not consider himself a good athlete and had only come to USF because the owner of the grocery store he worked at had arranged an interview and accompanied him to Kuharich's office. The coach listened to the grocer talk about Henneberry, then turned to the player and said, 'Best I can do for you is tuition. You'll have to buy your own books.' So, with one year of high school football, Henneberry became a running back on the USF freshman squad, popular with all the players because of his ever-present smile and his willingness to help them with their studies.

"But that day, I passed the empty seat next to Henneberry and stepped down the narrow aisle, holding onto the overhead straps, avoiding tripping over the large feet spreading across the walkway. I thought the seat next to Marchetti was still empty because there was little room to sit after Marchetti had settled his bulk next to the window. I had seen Gino drive up on his motorcycle and wrestle the bike to a secure lock-up next to the dorm. I'd heard the coaches talking about him. He was hard to miss at 6'6" and probably 230 pounds. If his size hadn't made him stand out, his age and dress would have..."

As I moved toward Gino, I heard a hum spreading down the aisle as word was passed from the front seats, where the coaches were sitting. This year the pre-season camp would be held in Corning. This meant nothing to most of the players, but by the time we passed through Oakland, they had heard incorrectly that it was in the central valley near Fresno, just off U.S. 99. As we continued inland, the windows of the bus were lowered at almost every seat, and the players became sure of one thing: Corning would be hot.

I stopped next to Gino's seat. "Mind some company?" Slouching there in the window seat, Gino was dressed in Levi's and a leather jacket with an improbable number of zippers. Years later, before Gino's Hall of Fame induction, I asked him about that jacket. He said it had sixteen zippers and they were a sign: the more zippers, the tougher the guy.

As I glanced down, I saw that what I had taken to be an empty seat was actually occupied by a scuffed green duffel bag that looked like it was from a cut-rate army surplus store. Marchetti glared at me, then at the bag. He had a growth of dark beard starting but had probably shaved that morning. It would have taken me a week to grow something so impressive. Looking up at me, Gino stood, ducking under the overhead storage rack and moving out into the aisle. With one hand, he picked up the duffel and stuffed it into the rack, forcing it into a space that would not have accepted it but for the malleable canvas of the bag and the strength of the hand pushing it.

Gino had played football the previous year in junior college, only because it allowed him to play with his brother. He was raw, not having played in high school. I was beginning to think approaching him had been a mistake when Marchetti levered himself back into his seat and gestured with an immense hand for me to take the seat beside him.

I shot out my hand as he sat down, and Marchetti enveloped it in his own.

"I'm Pete."

Marchetti nodded, and I thought he was not going to say anything at all. He looked out at the passing scenery, then back at me. "You must be important. Coach introduced you longer than any of the others."

I heard nothing from Marchetti for the next fifteen minutes. He sat quietly, looking out the window. It got hotter with each passing mile. The bus continued up the freeway through Berkeley, San Pablo, and Vallejo. The window to Gino's left started halfway back in our seating area. Marchetti had it opened fully, but all the air was going to the seat behind, where Dick Colombini, a reserve halfback and lineman, had his hand up, acting as a funnel, bringing what breeze there was directly into his face. Marchetti suddenly stood, bent at the waist and leaned over the bench in front of him. He slammed the window open, heard the locks click, then sat back down.

"They're wrong, you know. Corning isn't near Fresno. It's up near Chico, west of Sacramento. I rode through it last summer on my bike." I had heard Gino lived in Antioch, about thirty miles east of where we were traveling. The temperature there during summer was just as hot but with a higher humidity level, being closer to the Bay.

I decided I'd try to get him to open up a little more. "I grew up in Southern California, and I've driven up to San Francisco lots of times," I said. "I take 99 because it's faster than 101. It's always hot in summer. Open the windows, it cools the inside, but then dehydration sets in, which is why every fifteen miles or so I end up stopping at an Orange Julius refreshment stand."

"Corning will be hot," said Marchetti, though he actually didn't mind the heat. As I later learned, he liked riding his bike during the hot days; the open window now blowing hot air into his face must have reminded him of that. He would often sing out loud on the bike, risking swallowing a butterfly or a bug.

I knew that Marchetti hadn't finished high school before coming to USF, and I figured it might just be worth a story. "So how was it that you didn't finish high school?" I ventured. "How did that happen?"

Marchetti glared at this, and I thought for a second that I'd made a big mistake. Gino kept silent, nailing me with a look that seemed to search my face for some evil intent.

"It's not a bad thing," I added quickly, hoping I hadn't brought up bad memories for the big man sitting next to me. "I didn't have time to turn around after high school. I was on a ship in the Pacific before the ink on my diploma dried. Funny thing is, I tried to enlist in the navy three times. Each time I was rejected, not because I was too young—I sat out a year to work on my uncle's farm and was already eighteen—but because I was color-blind. Then, the same week I graduated from high school, I got my draft notice. It directed me to the recruiting center in L.A. I was just standing there in the back of a line that stretched around the building. It was moving slowly when one of the recruiters came out from a side door, pointed at me, gave me fifty cents, and asked me to go to the store and get him a quart of milk. He told the guy behind me in line to hold my place. I took the guy's money, got the milk, and knocked on the side door the recruiter had come from. He thanked me, took the change, and waved me inside, where he asked which service I'd like to join. I said navy, and navy it was. They never checked me for colorblindness. All the rest of the guys called in that day went to the army. A couple weeks later I was on a ship in the Pacific Ocean."

My story seemed to soften the muscles in Marchetti's face and his eyes went back to the window. For a minute I thought I was going to get the silent treatment again, but then, without moving his eyes from the window, Marchetti spoke. "I graduated from high school in a deal that let me enlist in the army a little early." Once that was out, he relaxed and told me about the war and his family.

"My mom and dad immigrated from Tuscany to West Virginia. Dad worked in the coal mines. During the Great Depression he moved the family here to Antioch. My brother Angelo—Lino, we call him—and I went to high school here. When the war was a couple years old, some government officials came to our house. Even though my dad had earned his citizenship years before, my mom was busy raising two boys and she hadn't. The government hassled my mom. The fact that she was Italian with a heavy accent caused trouble for the family. We were forced to move from our home to an apartment outside the city limits, with restrictions on her movements.

"My father taught us to love this country. Lino and I took it upon ourselves to make sure the government had no reason to further question our family's loyalty. So when he got out of high school, Lino joined the army. Two years later I followed him, and two months later I was at the Battle of the Bulge. They made me a machine gunner, mostly because I was able to handle the heavy gun like it was a rifle. No one ever thought to question my age.

"But if you really want to know why I'm at USF ... in France, I made friends with a guy named Jimmy De Palo. Jimmy had been drafted out of college. He was a year older than me. Most of our time at the front lines was spent waiting in the trenches, giving us a lot of time to talk. Both of us were scared shitless of the times we'd be ordered to move forward. Before the command, the noise level would increase to an almost unbearable level. First came the airplanes that would strafe the Germans. Others higher up could be seen circling, protecting the low-level assault planes from German fighters that were sure to come. Then the artillery shells would start flying just over our heads to land among the enemy's positions. After ten minutes of shelling it was hard to imagine that anything could have survived, but of course they did. When the sergeant's command came to move forward, we would cross ourselves and slip out of the ditch.

"Jimmy spent a lot of time telling me what he planned to do after the war. It was nervous talk, trying to lessen the tension in the trench. He wanted to get through the war, then finish college." Marchetti turned and looked Rozelle right in the eye. "College was the last thing on my list, although I was with Jimmy on the getting through the war part. News travels fast through the lines and rumor was that General George Patton was trying an end run around the Siegfried Line. It was January, and it was cold as hell in the trenches. The Germans responded with an all-out offensive, which we held off, at least in our section of the front. Twelve days before the war ended, Jimmy was standing next to me when he bought it from a piece of shrapnel. I had his brains and part of his helmet on my shoulder. Two years after I got home, in honor of my buddy, I enrolled in J. C."

In junior college, Gino first played football. His brother Angelo had played the year before, and the coaches at USF knew a lot more about him than about Gino. I had been told that it was Angelo Coach Brad Lynn had first thought to recruit.

The thought of De Palo seemed to turn Gino's faucet off. He didn't want to talk about the war anymore. He gazed at the miles of flat farmland that make up California's central valley, smelling the dry hay growing right up to the sides of the highway. I looked past Gino at the flat landscape that stretched for miles. In my drives over the Grapevine into the central valley from L.A., it was not hard to envision that it had once been a great inland lake stretching four hundred miles north to south and in places a hundred miles east to west. I waited for Gino to continue, but quiet as the land we were driving through, Gino spoke not another word.

It took five hours and two bus stops to arrive in the little farming town of Corning, where the team would be staying. This gave me time for more interviews, potentially. Coach Lynn had mentioned to me that Hal Sachs was a guy with an interesting background; I wondered how he could be more interesting than Marchetti. Unfortunately, Sachs was sitting next to the quarterback, Ed Brown. Two kids from Southern California, they were the same size, dressed the same, and kept up an animated conversation, laughing and slapping hands during most of the trip. I had to be content sitting next to the quiet Marchetti, writing the perfect human interest story in my head.

No one was sure what to expect from the camp in Corning. I planned to use the players' free time to get a cache of human interest stories while the players gradually worked themselves into condition. I knew how newspapers worked. If the team was good, it would get press, but they would need to fill the game accounts with interesting fluff. It was my job to provide it in a way that would make the players popular for more than their play. I had already struck gold with Marchetti. I had to see if I could do as well with the others.

The bus pulled into Corning and up to the entrance of the Rancho Tehama Motel. Across the street in the window of a grocery store, a large thermometer registered 115 degrees.

Today the NCAA regulates the hours of pre-season practice, as well as the conditions the student athletes practice under. In the professional ranks, the players' union and common sense, as well as restrictions from this office, dictate how hard the coaches are allowed to practice their players. Medically, so much more is known now about the human body and the way a pre-season camp should be run. In short, what happened during those two weeks at Corning would never be allowed now. In those years, it was all about tough men making it tough on their players to make them into tough men. Looking back on the conditions at Corning, it's a wonder someone didn't die. Kuharich hoped to mold the players into a cohesive team while getting them into the best condition of their lives. The players were there because they didn't know any better. This was their coach's training camp and if they wanted to be on the team, to play college football, then this was the price. In his Hall of Fame speech, Gino said it was the hardest two weeks of his entire life, that he had constantly been on the verge of quitting—and he'd been at the Battle of the Bulge.

The team piled off the bus with their bags and filed into the lobby of the motel. The assistant coaches went to reception to get keys to the rooms. Bud Kerr and Jim Ryan took turns going into the crowd of players and calling them two at a time, handing them their keys and room assignments, then returning to the counter for another set of keys.

Before the first pair left, Kuharich called for their attention. That oddly high-pitched voice rose in pitch as he increased his volume. Odd as it was, it could be heard the length of the football field. In the confines of the reception area, it seemed to bounce off the walls and the squares of marble tile floor that weren't covered with suitcases and gear.

"Back in the lobby in half an hour. That's three o'clock for those who have watches. Workout gear—full pads."

I was one of the last to be given a key and found that I was paired with Brad Lynn, the freshman coach, in the room next to Scrap Iron Young. Scrap Iron roomed alone, partly because his medical gear and training equipment filled the other half of his room. I was to find out that night that the other reason Scrap

Iron had his own room was his snoring, which was legendary. It pierced walls every bit as well as Kuharich's voice did.

While Brad got dressed in his coaching gear, I took a shower, which I badly needed after the five-hour ride. I put on a short-sleeved shirt, a pair of shorts, and a hat to help with my increasingly high forehead, and grabbed a notebook and pen, completing what amounted to my gear. I was ready to interview the players during their breaks and down time. By the time we finished the ten-minute walk to the football field, I needed another shower. I also discovered that I could have left the notebook and pen at the hotel.

Kuharich showed the team a preview in that first practice of what was to come for the next two weeks. It was after three-thirty in the afternoon by the time everyone was on the field. He started by sending the entire team around the field for two laps, a half-mile. Then he had the linemen do drills on the block-ing sleds while the ends did wind sprint routes with Brown and Henneberry throwing pass after pass.

The running backs and defensive backs ran forty-yard dashes with Coach Kerr keeping a record of their times. After an hour, the coach took the players through a series of push-ups, sit-ups, and jumping jacks before sending them around the track for another half-mile. After five minutes on the field, the players' jerseys were soaked with sweat. At ten minutes, the players started looking for water; there was none. When they asked about water, Scrap Iron rubbed his oft-broken nose with his index finger and told them he must have forgotten it, then that it was bad for them. It was a prologue to the conditions the team would train under for the following two weeks, when if anything, the afternoon temperatures got even hotter. By the end of the two-hour session, the players' jerseys were bone-dry but crusted with salt, the thick cotton fabric stiff from the accu-mulated white layer.

It was a weary bunch of players who trudged back to the hotel that evening. The Rancho Tehama hotel had been chosen for its affordability, as had Corning itself; the motel was not air conditioned. If anything, it was hotter inside than outside, especially in the rooms facing west. It was like getting into a car that had been out in the sun with its windows closed. The reality set in after the players had taken their showers: this would be a training camp beyond all their previous experiences.

There are two types of men—those who put their clothes in the drawers and those who live out of their suitcases. I was part of the first group. Everyone opened their windows and left their rooms, leaving the doors open, hoping for some sort of breeze to provide relief from the heat. Then they congregated in the lobby, which was several degrees cooler, and waited for dinner.

All the meals were served in the hotel. That first night they had steak and potatoes with greens and a sweet, sticky lemon square, but only St. Clair had any appetite, and he kept trying to have the waiter bring him raw steak. At first the waiter thought he was kidding, but finally, after the third try, St. Clair stood up, all 6' 8" of him towering over the poor guy, and offered to go back to the kitchen and personally instruct the cook. The waiter scurried away, practically running toward the kitchen. He returned almost immediately, as it didn't take long to prepare raw steak. As he was about to enter the dining area, he was stopped by Joe Scudero, who substituted the two baked potatoes on St. Clair's plate for two raw ones he had just obtained from the kitchen. The harried waiter hurried through the door with a gigantic raw slab of beef and Scudero's raw potatoes.

The Saint was not pleased as he cut into the potato, shaking his head and asking the rest of his table, "Do I look like I would eat a raw potato? Who would eat a raw potato?" Then he demolished the equally raw steak. Almost everyone in hearing laughed, and a chant began: "Geek, geek, geek!"

Although no one was particularly hungry after that first afternoon workout in the heat, it didn't stop them from drinking glass after glass of milk, iced tea, and water. Something the players didn't expect was a large bowl of iced olives on each table. Those who drank milk found the combination didn't click, the liquid the olives were preserved in curdling any milk that was still in their mouths. Those who drank the iced tea found the salty tartness of the olives delicious. By the second day, there were two bowls on each table, and even so, they were gone by mid-meal. Each day there seemed to be a different type of olive served, some as big as lemons. Those players who preferred milk started drinking it only after eating the olives.

After dinner, the players split according to position and were given a short lecture on the techniques they would be working on the following day. Then there was an optional movie, after which came bed call at 10:15. As the week progressed, most players by-passed the movie, hitting bed early, often dreaming of the cooling fog and sea breezes of San Francisco.

Sleeping called for another adjustment. It just didn't cool down as night fell. Kuharich announced that the team would walk to the field and be there at 9 am. Breakfast would be served at 7:30, lunch at 12:30, and the afternoon practice would start promptly at 2:30 pm. Most of the players, understanding what they were facing, tried to get to bed early. Most did not get to sleep easily, some not at all.

At two in the morning that first night, Burl Toler, a junior college transfer from San Francisco City College and a J. C. second-string All-American, after almost four hours of tossing and turning in the heat, remembered the marble tile in the entry area. Without waking his roommate, he took his pillow and went down the hall to the reception area. There was no moon that night and all the lights were off. As Toler moved into the lobby, he tripped over the prostrate form of Joe Scudero, who had already staked his claim on the tiles along with several other teammates who had thought of it hours before Toler. Toler got five-and-a-half hours that night and a full eight hours on subsequent evenings as more than half the players joined the first night's group. The rooms became more bearable in subsequent days as the players left the windows and doors open so when they returned for lunch and dinner, the rooms hadn't been baking in the sun without air circulation. This made for cooler sleeping temperatures, at least when compared to the first night's horror.

The first workout might have dulled their appetites the first evening, but the players made up for it in the morning. They ate scrambled eggs, bacon, and fried potatoes, along with porridge, Wheaties, and Grape-Nuts Flakes, and went back for seconds, then thirds. The hotel staff stared wide-eyed as the players devoured tray after tray of eggs and potatoes. Even the toast section had to be replenished again and again. To the staff's relief, the dining room was empty by 8:30 as the players left for their fifteen-minute walk to the field.

One of the coaches found a pipe platform that raised Kuharich about six feet above the surface of the field. He started practice every day with the players doing a half-mile run followed by fifteen minutes of stretching. This would take just under half an hour, and then he would split the squad up for drills, the quarterbacks and running backs practicing hand-offs for slants and end-arounds, the linemen on the blocking sleds. Everyone was in full pads and helmets.

Kuharich had been an All-American lineman for Notre Dame under the legendary Knute Rockne, and he had taken his own college coaches' practice schedules as guides and made them tougher. As the first days passed, he took to adding new wrinkles to the routine. He was bound and determined to bring his squad back to San Francisco in the best shape of their lives. One thing was consistent throughout the two weeks: the coach believed in full-speed hitting, two-a-days, and no water. On the second day, because of the players' continued requests for water, Kuharich did provide a pail of water. However, he filled it with oats, which soaked up the water. The players could partake, but it was impossible to swallow. The best you could do was press the mixture between your cheek and the sides of your teeth in the hopes of forcing some moisture out. After attempting this once or twice, the players gave up and suffered. Then Kuharich introduced the "Pit."

CHAPTER FIVE

I was learning the team slowly. There was not much free time in the morning or between practices, and the first few nights the players were so tired that they were in bed as soon as the sun set. I had short talks with several of them, just enough to get them familiar with me being around. I kept looking for a chance to sit down and talk with Harold Sachs, as Coach Lynn had suggested. He was a very handsome young man, tall with a physique that would have allowed him to excel in any sport he had chosen. He also looked older than many of the other players and was very popular with his teammates.

The town center of Corning was barely three blocks long. By the third evening the players had explored the whole of it. I left the hotel with a group of players, including Ollie Matson, who had tried to get Burl Toler to join him. Burl begged off because he wanted to read and the only time the hotel was quiet was after lights out or when the team was roaming the streets.

There was an ice cream parlor, complete with wire back chairs and brown Bakelite seats. Three small round tables, each surrounded by three chairs, were clustered around the front window. Three smaller versions lined the wall across from the soda counter, where the owner and his two daughters hurried to keep up with the orders. I was just about to order when I saw Sachs come in with Ed Brown. Brown immediately went to the counter, smiling at the two girls. It was obvious from their blushes that this was not his first time in the store, and he was interested in more than an ice cream cone.

I saw my opportunity and walked over to Sachs. "Can I buy you a sundae?"

"Sure," he answered.

"Can we have a ..."

"Strawberry."

"A strawberry sundae and a banana split, please. We'll be sitting over there." I pointed to one of the small tables. The owner glanced at where I was pointing, then looked at his daughters, both of whom were completely engrossed in taking Brown's order and in no hurry to finish.

"Alice!" the man shouted. "A banana split and a strawberry sundae."

Reluctantly, Alice left Brown and started to fill the order, leaving her sister with the prize and looking unhappy about it. She was younger by a year and a half and was used to taking a back seat to Vivian, her older sister, but that didn't make it any easier, watching Vivian bat her eyes and look up at the tall young man who by now every girl in town knew was the team's quarterback. I shook my head, paid for our order, and moved toward the table.

Sachs and I sat down across from each other at the little table. We had been in the heat of Corning for three days now, and most of the players were sunburned. Sachs had come in with a deep tan, which had only darkened. He was not inclined to start the conversation, so I said, "I understand that we have something in common. I come from Southern California as well."

"I'm from Chicago," he said with a thick Chicago accent, then looked away while I, only with supreme concentration, kept my mouth from dropping open.

He didn't say anything else until a lineman named Vince Tringali came by. "Yo, Vince. Heard you destroyed Gino in the Pit today."

Tringali pulled his hand back and glared at Sachs. I had started to hear the players talk about the Pit, but I had not yet been to the back of the south end zone, spending most of my time with the backs and receivers and watching Sachs kick extra points and field goals. As Tringali moved away, I noticed a large bruise on his left bicep and a slight limp that he was trying to disguise.

Alice came to the table with the orders. Sachs smiled as she set down his three-scoop strawberry sundae in front of him.

"Thank you, Alice," he said without a trace of the Chicago accent but with a smile that showed a perfect set of teeth, almost pure white in contrast with his deep tan. Alice smiled back, some of the sting of not having a fair chance at the quarterback lessened by the fact that this good-looking boy with the great smile knew her name.

I looked at him. He pointed at me and laughed, a deep, resonating, open-mouthed laugh.

"I was born in Chicago but we moved to San Clemente when I was ten, at the start of the war. You could say I'm from Southern California."

Several of the nearby players laughed at the trick he'd played on me. I had been had, but I didn't mind. Either I'd been accepted as part of the team or I was considered a joke. Over the next ten minutes Sachs told me his background, and I knew I had been accepted.

Hal Sachs had taken to the beach as soon as he arrived in San Clemente. He knew how to swim already, which was good since all his new friends were already surfing. He was big for his age and took to the ocean like a fish. By twelve he was body surfing, having graduated from a skimboard, and he was learning to ride a board in short order. The beaches from Dana Point in San Juan Capistrano south to the northern part of Camp Pendleton were not yet crowded, as they would become after the *Gidget* and *Endless Summer* films. The old guys like Dave Tansey, who worked as lifeguards for 50 cents an hour and surfed every minute of their time off, were teachers and mentors to the youngsters, and Sachs was one of their favorites. By the time he was seventeen, he was lifeguarding himself. The police chief, Art Denari, ignored the fact that Hal was under-aged. The lifeguards of San Clemente reported to the chief through their captain, who recorded times for all his crew. At the time that Hal joined, the captain was Tommy "Opie" Wert, who was an English teacher at Orange Coast College. He retired from teaching so that he could surf more and gave the captain position to Marv Crummer. Crummer probably pulled two hundred people out of the surf during rough water. In one afternoon alone, he made fourteen rescues. Unlike most of the piers to the north, San Clemente Pier had pilings that were close together. If anyone was caught beneath them, it could only turn out badly. Hal Sachs was credited with being the first to surf through them. At the time the boards were made of balsa wood covered in fiberglass, and they were big. To get an eleven-foot board through that maze took a lot of courage and great control. Some of the old-timers were still surfing with hollow plywood boards, with corks to let the water drain.

Hal's strength was a great advantage. At 6'2" and over 200 pounds and without an ounce of fat, he had superb balance and reflexes for such a large man. He would even take girls out on his board and ride tandem, lifting them up, something that not everyone was capable of doing.

Those forties and fifties lifeguards were a special group. Almost all went to college, most playing sports, and they became engineers, physicists, and businessmen. Hal Sachs went to the University of San Francisco to play center, linebacker, and place-kicker on the 1950 and 1951 football team, earning a degree in Business Administration.

CHAPTER SIX

It was still light, but the elevator down the hall from the NFL offices had considerably decreased its trips to the ground floor. Inside, Rozelle had freshened the drinks for both himself and Kensil. He lay back in his chair and crossed his feet on the desk.

"Whenever anyone asks one of the players about that year, the camp at Corning is the first thing they mention. It seemed to be both the hardest thing they ever endured and the single most important unifying factor in their becoming a team. When a man like Gino Marchetti admits to being done in by the camp, you know it was a bastard. In truth, it was more than that. I told you it was hot. It was more than hot. Something easterners don't fully realize is that in California, it stops raining in May and doesn't rain a drop until after Halloween. No afternoon thunder showers, no break from the heat, just day after day of sun. Those two weeks the temperature during the day never dropped below 107 degrees. At night it sometimes got down to eighty. There wasn't a space on the tile floor of the reception area that wasn't staked out for sleeping by the third night..."

The first week, the routine during the day never varied. On the field by 9. Twenty minutes of stretching and calisthenics, then a half-mile run around the track, followed by wind sprints. That took up an hour, after which the team was split up into squads according to position. Then the last hour, they scrimmaged—hard, full-contact scrimmage, with Coach standing on that raised platform, screaming at anyone who wasn't going full bore.

It was the same in the afternoon except the linemen, the blocking backs, and the linebackers were sent to the Pit after the stretching and run. The Pit was well named. I watched it on the fourth day. It had started the afternoon of the second day but I was watching the backs. Whoever thought it up must have been a sadist. What they did was this: they put two large tractor tires on the ground, lying on their sides with about four feet between them. A post was driven into the ground at their center, holding them in position. By the second day there was already a deepening gouge of dirt between the two tires. I watched the squad divide in half and line up on either side of the Pit. I was standing next to Bud Kerr, the line coach, who supervised the mayhem. I had heard the players complaining of the Pit, but I was still unprepared for what happened. Coach Kerr blew his whistle and then pressed his stopwatch. At the sound of the whistle blast, the men facing each other at the front of each line threw themselves toward each other. The sound of the collision was sickening, but the initial contact was just the start. Each player tried to force the other up and out of the Pit. Everyone was in full gear and helmets, which was good, because they battled each other with punches, kicks, and head butts. Anything to get an advantage and push their opponent back to his line of players.

Coach Kerr blew his whistle again after sixty seconds, the two players disengaged and went to the end of the line, and the next two stepped forward, waiting for Kerr's whistle. There was nothing held back—punches, kicks, slashes at heads and knees. If not for the full pads and helmets, there would have been serious injuries. It was the most brutal display of aggression I had ever seen.

It was the third trip through the line for Vince Tringali. As he advanced to where there were five people left in front of him, he scanned the opposing line and froze. He would again be facing Gino Marchetti. He looked down and discovered that his shoelace was not tied tightly on his right shoe. He stepped out of line, bent over, and retied the shoe, motioning for the player behind him, Roy Giorgi, to move up and take his place. His shoe now properly tied, he moved back into line, now in sixth place. Moving up, his face drained as he saw Giorgi throw himself into the pit against Lou Stephens, with Marchetti looking at him and smiling across their grappling bodies. Stephens had seen his move and told Gino, who had moved back as well. Marchetti was twenty-five years old, large and muscular, hardened by the war and by physical labor. He could be polite and deferential, but he had a mean streak that most of the time he kept well under control. This was not one of those times.

Coach Kerr blew the whistle, which took Giorgi and Stephens out of the Pit. Tringali looked down and saw fresh blood in the dirt of the hole that had developed between the two tires and Giorgi holding his hand to his face, trying to stanch the flow of blood between his fingers. Tringali looked up at Marchetti, who said, "Let's have it, wise guy." The whistle blew and the two flew at each other. The players behind had caught word of what was going on and the lines were re-formed into two semi-circles behind the two men. Tringali knew he couldn't run; his only hope was all-out aggression. He drove hard at Marchetti's midsection, hitting it with all his weight and the drive of his legs on his own shoulder pad. Marchetti grunted but did not move, not even an inch. Instead, two massive fists came directly down on the smaller man's shoulder pads, followed by slaps to each earhole in his helmet. Dazed and completely out of answers, Tringali was hit on the legs, his arms thrust against the tire on the right, then on the left. He was grabbed before he was knocked out of the Pit, back to his own line, by a vicious forearm shiver. Tringali, on his knees, wrapped his arms around Marchetti's legs, hanging on for dear life as his shoulder pads were pounded with fists and elbows and his helmet bounced from left to right.

Coach Kerr watched the dial go past the usual sixty seconds, glanced at the mayhem that was going on in the Pit, and let the second hand slide for another thirty clicks. He had not seen Tringali's subterfuge or Marchetti's counter, but the players had never reacted like this before. Some matches had interested them, but none like this one. They were enjoying themselves, as was Marchetti. Tringali was getting pummeled, but Kerr liked the fact that he was still trying to fight back—not effectively, but with determination. Marchetti outweighed him by forty pounds, but after the first few seconds he had not really tried to injure the smaller man, just punish him, not allowing him out of the Pit, keeping him in to the delight of the surrounding players. Finally, Kerr blew the whistle and the carnage stopped. Tringali started to drop to his hands and knees, blood pouring from his nose and a cut on his left hand. Marchetti stopped his slow descent with an arm around Tringali, grasping him under his arms and lifting him effortlessly out of the Pit, saying in a loud voice, "Good match."

Behind him the whistle blew, and Toler and Colombini went at it, a mismatch as well, but not nearly as vigorous as the one before.

The cheers and cat calls had brought coach Brad Lynn to the Pit, where he watched the end of Marchetti's demolishing of Tringali. As Kerr motioned the next two in, Lynn said to me, "I never told you the story of recruiting Gino, did I?"

He walked me down the field about ten yards. "You know I was first interested in his brother, Angelo. He was good, though not as good as a lot of the players we had already signed. But Gino. Gino was another story, so fast, so strong. I went to his house to talk to him, but his parents told me he was bartending in a local place not far away. It was a local place—bar, pool table, and a couple of tables. I was overdressed again in a suit and tie, which had a table of regulars looking at me as if I was there to serve a warrant. Gino was behind the bar in a T-shirt with a pack of cigarettes rolled up the sleeve. He didn't recognize me at first, but as I made my way toward him, I saw understanding cross his face and he threw the cigarette he was smoking beneath the bar. I told him about USF and offered him the scholarship, but I told him that he should stop smoking. He accepted right there and was signing the letter of intent on top of the bar when fire flamed up from under the counter where he had thrown his butt. I snatched up the paper and Gino put out the flames with the soda nozzle. Best signing I ever did. Even the locals at the bar applauded."

After the Pit, the players most often recalled the heat and lack of shade. For three hours each morning and afternoon, the relentless sun beat down on the players in full workout uniforms. Scrap Iron would collect the jerseys and socks at night. He had found a laundromat, which at least washed out the crusted salt from the tops and the stink from the socks and underwear. It wasn't for cleanliness. Kuharich had noticed abrasive sores showing up under their arms, and most of the players were complaining of jock rot, so each morning the players would find their clean clothes outside their door.

The high school field was in an open area. There was no shade. During morning stretches and calisthenics, players would line up to the west of Bob St. Clair. Afternoon saw them to the east. Scudero and two others benefited from the shade provided by his six feet eight inches. It wasn't long before the squad noticed that there was a single telephone pole at the 30-yard line to the west. In the afternoon, as the sun lowered, this pole cast a thin line of shade across the field. It was not unusual to see a line of ten or more players, mostly ends and running backs, standing in the line of shade offered by the single pole and St. Clair, waiting for their turn to run their routes. Standing in that shade lowered the heat by at least ten degrees.

On Friday, the fourth day of full practice, Joe Scudero came up to Ollie Matson and said, "I've found something. Make like you're chasing me and I'll show you." With that, he juke-stepped past Matson, straight-armed him in the chest, and took off toward the north end zone. At the ten-yard line, he stumbled and fell to his knees, even though he was pulling away from Matson.

"Tackle me," he said as Matson continued to accelerate. As they both lay on the ground, Scudero motioned to a depression in the turf that was about the size of a football and filled with water left by the sprinkler that had been used on the grass during the early morning hours. Scudero cupped his hands and scooped up some of the liquid. Muddy as it was, he downed it in two swallows, giving up his position and hiding Matson's actions from the coaches. Ollie looked at the water, now swirling with dirt and cut grass, placed his hand under the surface, and repeated Scudero's action, then went back for it again.

"Let's keep this to ourselves. If the coaches find out about it, they'll be out here at 8:30 with sponges."

"What are you two doing?" came a high-pitched yell from the platform thirty yards away.

"Push-ups, Coach!" yelled back Scudero, who then did three quick push-ups, each time lowering his mouth to the puddle. Scudero stood up to his full five-six and trotted to the running back drill line, followed by a grinning Matson.

The lack of water was the Notre Dame way. What Kuharich failed to remember was that every hour they'd had a break where they could eat oranges and dip towels in water to wipe the sweat off their faces. He didn't remember wringing the wet towels into his mouth or chewing on them to get a little moisture, or that it had rained almost every summer afternoon in South Bend as well. They had played through it as long as there wasn't accompanying thunder and lightning. In Corning, there was none of that, only relentless sun with low humidity that evaporated your sweat as soon as it formed in an attempt to cool the body's core temperature. The players' bodies responded with severe cramping and vomiting. Scrap Iron's answer to cramping was to hit the cramping muscle to break the spasm and give the player heat fatigue salt pills left over from the navy in World War II. The pills were to be taken in the morning before practice and in the afternoon when the players were drinking gallons of iced tea.

The ultimate in cramping was experienced by Dick Colombini after his go with Toler and the scrimmage that concluded the afternoon workout. Walking back to the hotel, Colombini started to feel a cramp in his right foot. As he got to the hotel, it was hurting so much that he sat down on a chair in the reception area, unable to make it to his room. His ankles cramped, then both calves, followed by his hamstrings, his shoulders, and his arms. He became absolutely rigid. His cry for help brought Scrap Iron, who with help hefted the inflexible Colombini onto the training room table and started working the muscles out of spasm with a not-so-gentle massage. The cramps didn't break for almost an hour and a half. The next day, Colombini was excused from the drills, but continuous running around the track was substituted. Running would have been an incorrect term – limping was much more accurate.

Colombini had played running back for the freshman squad and was listed as such in his sophomore year, but just before camp, he had been called into Kuharich's office. He had noticed the speed and power of Ollie Matson and the quickness of Joe Scudero, and with Peacock as backup, he had seen the writing on the wall. He literally saw it when he entered the Quonset hut that acted as the main football office. On the blackboard behind Kuharich's desk were the names of all the players and a big X next to his name on the running back list. He was sure he was going to be cut. He was readying his response when the coach told him that he was going to move him from running back to guard and tackle and told him to bulk up ten pounds. He had to learn a new position both on offense and defense. He was in Corning knowing that he had to compete for the position if he wanted to stay on the team, and being laid up with cramps made him nervous. There was no way he was going to miss practice the next day. He ran slowly, hobbling around the oval, but kept it up until told to stop.

Colombini had entered the camp weighing 210 pounds. After the fourth day, he had lost fifteen pounds and was just under 195. He was built like his father, strong rather than rangy, powerful rather than supple. His teammates thought he used free weights to build his body. He didn't, of course. He had grown his muscles lifting bales of hay and blocks of ice. But that day in Corning, regardless of their origin, it seemed that every muscle took it upon itself to seize into a tight ball.

Colombini's father, Egidio, had come to America at sixteen and moved to Sonoma, sixty miles north of San Francisco. He joined his brother, who had arrived years before, eventually marrying and having Richard. Like most Italians, he faced discrimination, not only because of Italy's role in both wars but also because he was an immigrant. Fortunately, in rural Sonoma County, things were less intense than in the big cities. Egidio was a strong man and made his own way with only minor incidents. However, he noticed the unfairness inflicted on others and taught his family not to indulge in such acts of idiocy. He also taught his son that once he took on a job, he should never give up and should give his all to the man he worked for.

In later years, Scrap Iron admitted he had forgotten that Colombini was running laps. He had wanted the player to run a little to loosen up, then do some stretches. He knew that the lineman would be all but crippled from the previous day's cramps.

The team was two hours into morning practice, about to run scrimmages, and he saw the kid still lapping the field, limping in a painful shuffle. He made up for his neglect by sending Colombini back to the hotel to tell the kitchen to prepare double the amount of iced tea, instructing him to wait at the hotel till the team arrived for lunch. Scrap Iron laughed when he told Coach Kuharich about sending Colombini back early after forgetting about him running the track for an extra two hours. Kuharich accused him of getting soft.

CHAPTER SEVEN

Corning is located in the northwest Central Valley of California. It is typical of many small towns spread across the length and breadth of what was once a great inland sea. In 1950 it owed its existence to the farm community it served, not to any larger town that might be nearby. Corning is situated between Chico to the southeast and Red Bluff to the north but is not tied to them either economically or culturally. It had more of an allegiance to the railroad that ran through town and the farmers who worked the farms clustered around it than to those two small cities. The state capital of California, Sacramento, just over a hundred miles away, was a destination rather than a neighbor.

Kuharich had chosen Corning not because of its isolation, although it certainly was isolated, nor because of its heat, which it certainly had. In fact, he was not expecting the extreme temperatures that hovered over the practice field for those two weeks, which averaged ten or more degrees higher than normal. He hoped the team would not discover that the Chico State coach had moved his pre-season practice site toward the coast to escape the heat that Kuharich had chosen for his team. As much as anything, he had chosen Corning because it was cheap. This was not Notre Dame with their stadium, two dedicated practice fields, and virtually unlimited budget. There was no way he could feed his players at home for as little as he could at the Hotel Tehama. Also, the baseball team at USF did not take kindly to the destruction that two-a-days caused their shared turf and had complained to Father Dunne the year before. They were also fond of complaining about the blood on the grass. During the summer, the USF campus virtually shut down as well. It was good to change scenery. It helped to keep the players concentrated on training with no distractions.

The business district of Corning was three blocks long, filled with farm supply stores, a bar or two, a tractor showroom, a five-and-dime variety store, three cafes, and two churches, neither of them Catholic. The five-and-dime, the bars, and the ice creamery were the only places that interested the young men of USF. On the other hand, everything about the team interested the townspeople, especially the girls of Corning. With so many young men being taken by the draft or enlisting in the armed services for the Korean War, the girls outnumbered the boys almost three to one. Having thirty-nine good-looking young athletes placed at their disposal was almost too good to be true. Unfortunately, the coaches kept the boys on the field almost all day and gave them a curfew that put them in bed much too early. Sunday was understood to be a day of rest, so most of the players were looking forward to Saturday night and the girls of Corning even more so.

Kuharich cut the Saturday practice by an hour and a half, calling the players around him at the center of the field. He was not one for speeches, but in truth he was more than satisfied with the team's effort during the first six days. He knew if he could sustain the effort for the following week, he would be bringing the team back to San Francisco in the best shape of their young lives. He also knew that once they survived Corning, they would be able to overcome any adversity. He stood, not on his platform but in their midst, his high voice solid with authority.

"I'm sure all of you want to be champions as much as I do. You are USF Dons, and you could become champions. For those who don't know, a don is a Spanish nobleman with a sword in

A MORAL STANCE

his hand and religion in his heart. What I see in front of me this week is raw material, but material that with dedication and training could become a team of dons. A winning team must be strong, resilient, and flexible. But more than anything it must be cohesive, a team well prepared to impose its collective will on an opponent. This week was intended to give you strength and endurance to achieve that goal. Next week we will install the plays during scrimmage that will help you to win. But know for certain that it will not be the plays or the individual players that will succeed. It will be the team. I promise you, you will leave here that team. Tomorrow—Sunday—you have off. Tonight I am extending curfew by two hours, until midnight. Don't take advantage. Scrap Iron will do bed check."

After an early dinner provided by the hotel, Matson, Peacock, Colombini, Scudero, and St. Clair were walking around downtown, drinking soda and telling jokes. They saw Brown and Tringali coming out of the five-and-dime, both having donned brand new 59-cent straw hats. Scudero started it by laughing at them and calling them "locals." Pretty soon everyone but Matson had joined in ribbing the two. Just then, a group of young girls turned the corner, noticing the boys, especially Brown, whose smile was even more enchanting under his new lid set at a jaunty angle. Ever the playboy, he began to talk with them, and soon he was walking down the street with the girls. One of them play-fully adjusted Tringali's new hat to just the right rake as Tringali caught up with his quarterback. The group of mockers watched this scene unfold without surprise, knowing Brown, but mar-veled that the attention had extended to Tringali, who was not the best-looking of men. They decided to go inside the five-and-dime and get hats for themselves.

It stayed light until after eight, and the temperature remained in the high seventies well past dark. As evening progressed, many of the players, especially the juniors and seniors, who were of

47

age, ended up in the bar located nearest the ice cream parlor. Ed Brown and Tringali were sitting in a booth, sharing drinks with three young women, laughing, flirting, and spending much of the money they had brought with them to camp. Brown pushed his new hat up off his forehead and looked at his watch. He motioned to Tringali and said, "We got to go."

"We got time for another round," said Tringali.

"You don't have to leave. It's still early," said one of the girls.

"I'll buy this one," said another.

Brown hesitated, seeming to weaken, but then said, "Sorry, duty calls. Come on, Vince. I have a feeling the Barracuda will be on the prowl tonight."

They got up and left the bar, motioning to several other groups of players and pointing to the clock on the wall. The girls they were flirting with, after voicing displeasure at their departure, pulled chairs up to join the other group and were welcomed gladly.

At the hotel, Kuharich, Kerr, Ryan, and Scrap Iron watched the clock approach midnight. Kuharich noticed a group of young men in the shadows walking across the field to the back of the hotel.

"Give them ten minutes past twelve and help Scrap Iron with the bed check. If some of them are not in their beds, check for them in the lobby and on the back porch," said Kuharich.

At the stroke of midnight, Scrap Iron, clipboard in hand, met with the other coaches in the lobby, impatient to start the bed check. Starting oddly enough at Brown and Tringali's room, he slowly opened the door, shining the light into the darkness to find them both lying in bed grinning at him. He shined the light along the floor.

"At least have the decency to take off your shoes." He made two checks on his sheet and went to the next room.

_____

The next morning before breakfast, the players were called to the front of the hotel. There were two players standing next to Kuharich with a car idling behind them, its back door open. As the team watched, the two players walked around the car, flanked by Coaches Kerr and Lynn. They were not allowed to speak to anyone and their eyes were downcast as they slid into the back seat and were driven away. Kuharich moved up onto the first step of the hotel entryway and turned toward the assembled players, who were watching the car depart.

"Football is a team sport. A team only functions if we are all on the same page. That only happens if everyone follows the same rules. A play will break down unless every one of the eleven players on the field does his job. If anyone else does not want to be part of this team, let me know now."

The players looked at each other, clearly uneasy at losing two of their friends. One of them, Gaylord Quart, was particularly popular. Tringali could not help but remember that Quart had been one of those in the bar when they had left. He took a deep breath and gave Brown a knowing look. There was more to being a quarterback than passing the ball.

The team filed slowly back to the dining room in groups, selecting tables, putting their hats down before heading to the breakfast buffet, which, it being Sunday, had a few new items on it.

St. Clair returned to the table, his plate loaded six inches high with eggs and potatoes. He took the end seat that had been left for him so he could stretch his legs out to the side. Already sitting were Matson, Tringali, Marchetti, Toler, and Scudero.

"I had a dream last night that something bad was going to happen," said St. Clair even before touching his food. "I kept hearing the Barracuda's voice: 'Produce or get out, you piece of shit,' just like he does on the field, only without the swearing. That's how I knew we were still in Corning—Coach cursed. Now we lose two guys. It could have been any of us."

"Calm down, big guy," said Matson. "It couldn't be us because we were back before check. Burl here didn't even go out. He just stayed in and read all night. Those guys broke the rules. It didn't take a genius to know that Scrap Iron would be on the prowl after Coach gave us two extra hours last night." Matson let his voice trail off, as if he was embarrassed at speaking so long.

"I know what Saint means," said Tringali. "I'm always being yelled at. If not by Kuharich, then by Kerr. The only time I get any praise is when I go out of control during scrimmage."

"You don't just go out of control, Vince. You go absolutely nuts out there. No one wants to be across the line from you. You keep it up after the whistle and use every dirty trick in the book. Do you just want to be noticed?" asked Marchetti.

"Noticed? I'm trying to get knocked out! That's the only way I'll get off that field. And what do I get for it? Compliments from the coaches. Damnit, I wanna get knocked out!"

"I'll tell you what," said Marchetti. "Vince wants to knock himself out. How crazy is that? This is bullshit! We're in the middle of a desert. No water, and that screech owl yelling at us for six hours a day. I never thought a week could last so long, and we have another week of it. The war was easier. At least I had a gun and could shoot myself if things got this bad. You wanna get knocked out? I just want out, period…today. I don't need this crap."

The table got quiet. Several tables surrounding them also stopped talking and turned, looking at Marchetti. At the coaches' table, only Brad Lynn turned, although Marchetti's voice was loud enough for all to hear what he had said.

"I said that I wanted to get knocked out, not that I wanted to leave," said Tringali. "I think what we need is some music to soothe the wild beast." He reached behind him and pulled his ever-present ukulele out of his backpack. He strummed a few chords and began to sing "Goodnight Irene," a ballad made popular by the Weavers folk music group. He was quite good on the instrument, and soon a lot of the players were singing along with him. More importantly, Marchetti's face faded from red to the natural pink most of the players had acquired from the sun.

I was eating with the coaches and watched Kuharich. It was as if the coach hadn't heard Marchetti's outburst or even the song that Tringali led in its aftermath. He just kept quietly eating. The assistant coaches followed his lead. After a while he took his plate up and came back to the table with a couple of extra Eggs Benedict, which had been added to the menu for this Sunday breakfast.

"Coaches' meeting at two," Kuharich said as he finished off the two eggs. "Rozelle, you don't have to come. Enjoy your Sunday."

CHAPTER EIGHT

"It's getting late and the story is getting long," said Rozelle across his desk to Jim Kensil, then turned and flicked the off switch on the tape recorder that was nearing the end of the reel.

"Pete, there's nothing I'd like better than to hear more about that '51 Dons team. Every year their record, their players, and their stand become more important. I know they didn't go to a bowl, but almost nobody could tell you who won the 1951 National Championship without looking it up. The fact that you were involved with the team is worth your weight in gold as PR. This is the best evening I've spent with you in a long time."

"Well, let's at least go get some dinner."

"Why not just order in?" suggested Kensil. "There's that Italian place on the next block. They deliver. I'll freshen our drinks."

"Okay. I sometimes forget myself what a great story it is. Usually I think about it in terms of giving me my big break, how important it was in my career. I should be reminded how important it was to those players and to football itself. The decision they made, and what they did with themselves later in life—how important it was to our nation as a whole."

Kensil walked to the bar, stopping to pick up Rozelle's empty tumbler. He freshened the drinks, this time adding a good measure of water to the scotch and ice, while Rozelle ordered food to be delivered. Then Rozelle resumed his story.

"That Sunday afternoon while the coaches were meeting, I felt excluded, but I began to realize the true extent of Joe Kuharich's loyalty. I came to understand the reason I was being left out of the meeting. I was not a coach. Kuharich knew exactly what he was doing with the team. He had isolated them and given them every reason to rebel. He wanted them to overcome that reaction and come together as a team as much as he wanted them to return to San Francisco physically fit. At USF, over half the team came from San Francisco and lived at home. Some, including Bob St. Clair, were even married. They had not had the opportunity to meld into a cohesive unit. Sure, they did that somewhat on the field, but not as a fully integrated team, invested in each other as individuals, with a total commitment off the field as well. This training camp was their best opportunity to become a team, a family. Kuharich had done the same thing with his coaching staff. Everyone had a strong background at Notre Dame. He had pieced the staff together carefully over the three years he had been head coach.

"I'd learned how inbred the staff was while having lunch with the coaches each day of the first week of camp. I was the wild card, the oddball in the group. I had come from basketball, I had no connection with Notre Dame. The only reason I was there, I was beginning to realize, was that they needed publicity. The team would win, but what good would it do if no one saw them, or worse, no one heard of them? The school relied heavily on the gate receipts to finance the program as well as the rest of the Athletic Department. Two years before, the 49ers, a professional football team, had come to San Francisco and stolen as much as eighty percent of the fans from the Dons. It had become more and more apparent that it was my job to reverse that trend and fill Kezar Stadium again. That was never a problem at Notre Dame. Motels sold twenty-year leases to particular rooms for each weekend of home games. And Kuharich was pure Notre Dame.

"Kuharich was born in South Bend and became an All-American guard and a member of the college all-star team that defeated the NFL-champion Washington Redskins in 1937. He was the Notre Dame freshman coach in 1939, then played professionally until 1941, when he made first-string all-pro for the Cardinals. The war interrupted his professional career and he went into the navy as a lieutenant. After the war and a brief resumption of his professional football career with the Pittsburgh Steelers, he joined USF as line coach in 1947. In 1948 the head coach left, and Kuharich was made head coach and began recruiting Notre Dame assistants.

"Some of this I knew already, but most of the information was given to me in bits and pieces by the assistants, because Joe did not often talk about himself. He started putting his staff together and with the addition of Brad Lynn began effectively recruiting.

"Brad Lynn was the freshman coach, but his real job soon became recruiting. He had graduated from Notre Dame in 1939 and had spent six years as an officer in the navy. He had a year coaching high school in Santa Cruz before Kuharich brought him to USF as backfield coach and freshman coach. He had recruited most of the players who were now at camp. To say he was good at recruiting would be a gross understatement. He had already told me about the recruiting of Hal Sachs, and I suspected there were good stories behind the recruitment of other players.

"Bud Kerr was another quiet man. He had also won All-American honors while at Notre Dame in 1939, and like Kuharich, he played in the all-star game and professionally. Kuharich had brought him in in 1949, shortly after he took over the team, and by 1950 the Dons were ranked fourth in the nation on defense, holding opponents to only 74.5 yards a game. That was a stat that would plague them in trying to convince other colleges to play them the following year.

"Even Scrap Iron Young was Notre Dame through and through. He had worked as a trainer at Notre Dame for twenty-three years. Because of his broken facial features and his primitive approach to training and injuries, most people were surprised to learn that he had graduated with a law degree from Notre Dame. His approach to injuries, 'Rub a little dirt on it,' melded nicely with Kuharich's 'Produce or get out,' which he would often yell at the players, especially the young Bob St. Clair.

"Only Jim Ryan, of all the coaches, did not have Notre Dame roots. He was solid USF, having been an award-winning quarterback in 1946. Now, not only did Kuharich have the players he wanted, but the coaching staff had two or three years of working together with the team to bring them to championship level. The trick would be to get them to pull together, to work as a unit.

"That first Sunday morning in Corning, Tringali's ukulele helped bring the team together, and Kuharich never said a word about Marchetti's outburst. It was as if he had never heard those words, but I suspect he heard them quite well. He had seen what a devastating force of nature Marchetti could become on defense, as Matson would be on offense. Scudero, working in tandem with Matson, was almost as effective serving as a change-of-pace scatback. Toler was the same to Marchetti's defense. They had the stars, but what excited Kuharich was that there were good players at every position, sometimes two deep. I made a mental note to talk to Coach Kerr about recruiting and have a serious conversation with Toler, who was seldom seen without a book in his hand and reading glasses in his shirt pocket."

Rozelle was interrupted by a knock on the door. He went to the door and let in the waiter who was delivering the food. It was not the first time he had delivered to the NFL offices, and he had brought plates, cloth napkins, and silverware. He set up the places on the coffee table in front of Kensil and announced the items: "Chicken parmesan, spaghetti, raviolis, and mixed veggies. I also brought you French bread and butter, sir."

Rozelle paid the man, adding a tip of almost 50%, and said, "Please pick up these dishes tomorrow morning. It looks great." Rozelle escorted him back through reception and out the door. On the way back, he stopped by the refrigerator that was under the bar and brought out a bottle of 1968 Château Margaux, expertly opening it and grabbing two glasses.

"I said that I wasn't invited to the coaches' meeting. That was not quite true. At three in the afternoon, Scrap Iron Young knocked on my door..."

"Coach wants to see you."

Scrap Iron led me to the small meeting room the hotel had provided for the coaches, as none of the rooms were big enough to accommodate the group. It was really only a normal-sized bedroom with the beds removed in favor of a table and chairs. All the coaches were still there, sitting around the table, looking relaxed.

"What's the mood out there?" asked Kuharich as Scrap Iron took the nearest seat, while I skirted the table. I sat down before answering.

"From what I saw and heard after you left, most of the players were intent on calming down the few who were upset. Henneberry, Tringali, and Sachs were particularly involved with Marchetti. Those who were griping the most seemed more upset about the conditions at workouts than about Quart's dismissal."

"Okay. We'll take care of it. That's not why I asked you to join us. I won't ask you to snitch on the players, although I might ask your opinion of the boys from time to time. Your job is publicity and to do that you need their trust. At the same time, anything you hear from me or the coaches is not to be talked about unless we say so. Is that understood?"

"Absolutely," I answered. I was just finished with being a student, and quite frankly, Kuharich scared the crap out of me. I saw him as having control over my future.

"We have been blessed with a confluence of destinies. The players who have just transferred in, added to those who came up from the freshman team that lost only one game last year, and those twenty who were on the roster last year, add up to a rare combination. They also present a problem for me. They are too good for what I had in mind this year. We were 7 and 3 last year. This year we should be better, much better. Problem is that everybody on the west coast knows it. If I get what I want out of this team, this year will be a development year, learning a whole new style to fit our personnel."

I looked over and saw Jim Ryan, the backfield coach, smiling, while Kuharich and Coach Kerr were absolutely serious.

"What we are is undersized in the line and oversized in the backfield and ends. Football games are won on the ground. Always have and always will be. At Notre Dame we were taught that only three things happen when you put the ball in the air, and two of them are bad. But Coach Lynn and luck have given me a core of players who will thrive in the passing game. We also have Matson and Scudero. They would make any run-oriented coach deliriously happy, but we don't have the linemen yet who can open holes for them. Heck, we have six players who didn't even play in high school, including Marchetti. You see my problem?"

I didn't, but I nodded.

"I have a quarterback with a cannon for an arm," said Kuharich. "Kid is destined for the pros. He has the finest group of receivers I've ever seen on one squad. Peacock, Ralph Thomas, and St. Clair will be great receivers if they synch with Brown in their routes. Even Matson and Scudero have shown sticky fingers in the drills last week. We have to pass. To do so I will have to develop a whole new playbook. Stop grinning, Ryan. You have the most work to do on that score. This is going to be harder on the coaches than the players.

"The main reason I brought you in here is that you must understand what we are trying to do and build excitement around it, but not too soon. It will take months to teach the players exactly what we want from them and make sure they feel comfortable with our scheme. I want you to understand what we are doing but not advertise it until it starts to click.

"This first week was to try and weed out the players who weren't serious and to get everyone used to hardship. This next week we start drills and technique. I'm not as worried about defense. With Matson roving around in the backfield, and Marchetti and Toler as linebackers or linemen, I doubt that many will score on us. It's the offense, particularly the line play, that will take time. Pump up Matson, Scudero, Marchetti, Toler, St. Clair, and Thomas. They can be the stars. They have the natural ability. The rest we have to make into stars."

CHAPTER NINE

Kuharich was true to his word. The intensity and daily schedule of the camp didn't change, but the coaching did. The players were still roused at 7 am for Mass at 7:30. Breakfast was at 8 am, but then instead of going directly to the field, the players were given individual skills practice tests using the blackboard. A play was placed on the board in chalk and under the eyes of the coaches, individual players were brought forward to scheme the route and assignment of every player on the board, not just their own position. After Monday, when several of the squad had shown less than complete knowledge of the plays, the players were much better prepared. At 9:45 everyone was on the field for an hour and a half for routes and scrimmage. It was still full contact, with everyone hitting, but it was not as monotonous as the first week. They practiced the plays and formations they had learned in the team meeting held the previous evening. Lunch was at 12:15, and then there were short afternoon lectures that concentrated on what they had been given the evening before, so practice didn't start again until 2:30. It gave them lots of time to rehydrate and digest lunch and the pounds of iced olives that had become a staple at every meal.

They were back on the field at 3:30 for a full two hours of drills and scrimmage. Kuharich was more often on the field demonstrating a technique to the linemen than on his perch on top of the platform, until the real scrimmage started. Then he resumed his place and the megaphone, constantly reminding the players on the field to "Produce or get out!" Players still sought shade, standing next to St. Clair or the telephone pole near the field.

The coaches could see the transformation in the players. They were no longer constantly trying to outdo each other. Instead they were helping each other with the techniques they had learned. If they had an opinion on the shift from run blocking to pass blocking, no one talked about it, but I thought the offensive linemen appreciated backing up rather than throwing themselves into the defensive line and getting pummeled by Marchetti, Thomas, and Tringali, who was still trying to get himself knocked out.

Dinner was at 6:45, followed by a critique of the day's performance, or if things had gone well in the eyes of the coaches, a short skull session where several new plays were drawn up and explained for the next day's scrimmage. A movie projector would be set up in the dining room and those who wanted to could watch a film that Kuharich had brought with him from San Francisco. Scrap Iron would act as projectionist. The movie over, Scrap Iron would be moving from room to room by 10:15 with his ever-present clipboard in hand.

Years afterward, when the players met for their many reunions, Corning was always brought up, even before they discussed the actual games. Sachs would always laugh that he had not been able to eat an olive since that week. He also laughed that a fifty-nine-cent straw hat had ever been considered the height of fashion. All agreed it was the toughest thing they had ever done, but most became philosophical about it with the passing of time.

"Kuharich knew how tough it was. He wanted it tougher than anything we would experience in the next few years. He wanted us to know that we could overcome anything," recounted Dick Colombini.

Every reunion, Dick Stanfel would recite, "No one believes the stories. They think it's fiction. No air conditioning. No water. The shade from one telephone pole. You became mean. You wanted to hurt someone."

Ed Dawson remembered that after Kuharich had seen Scudero at the sprinkler, he ordered the grounds crew to water only during the evening after they were through with practice, not in the morning. Scrap Iron mentioned to one of the players in passing that he thought beer had replaced many of the salts and nutrients he had provided. It had the ring of truth. A number of players would go to the store and buy beer, using it to wash down the four salt tablets he would give to each player every day. Some took two in the morning and two in the afternoon, but some waited until they got through with workouts so they could swill the dime-sized pills with the beer. The only problem was that after becoming so dehydrated, even one beer would give you a buzz, which meant you had to stay well away from Coach at dinner.

The team still ran wind sprints both morning and afternoon, which was brutal, but the drills concentrated on technique rather than speed. The backs particularly were being taught to read the line openings and not to rely on speed alone. This meant that the line had to get better at opening the holes. Lou Stephens was the biggest lineman at the guard position. He weighed as much as Marchetti and was thirty-five pounds heavier than Greg Hillig, who played on the opposite end of the line at left guard. Only Mike Mergen, who played behind Burl Toler at tackle, and St. Clair at end were bigger, and Mergen was not as quick off the snap. Kuharich drilled them on team blocking schemes, particularly those involving pulling guards. What the line gave up in size, they made up for in the techniques that they were learning.

Kuharich might have recognized that the talent he had lent itself to a passing game, but every instinct he had honed at Notre

Dame and in the pros told him to run the ball and run it vio-
lently, and Stephens became his whipping boy. Play after play was
run over his side of the line. Next to him at right tackle was Toler,
and to his right, St. Clair. Toler had only played a single year of
football at City College, but he was smart, and much more athletic than Stephens. Even when Toler made a mistake, his speed,
size, and strength often allowed him to make up for it. Then
either Kuharich or Coach Kerr would take him aside and go over
the technique with him. With Stephens, they just yelled. His only
solace was that if anything, Bob St. Clair was yelled at more.

With St. Clair, it was usually that he was not doing something downfield. He had been used to catching passes, not blocking downfield. On defense he was used to being physical, taking
advantage of his size and strength. As I mentioned earlier, his
problem with Scudero, who had come from Galileo—along with
Mission, Polytechnic's main high school rival—was from a play
when St. Clair was playing the defensive left end position. He had
almost taken the little running back's head off with a clothesline
tackle in the high school championship game. The little guy was
only out for three plays, but the rest of the game he couldn't see
out of his right eye and got blindsided a couple of times. Scudero
thought it was a dirty play, but it wasn't; well, maybe a little bit,
since St. Clair hit him with his fist. Now that they were on the
same team, the quick little running back still had not forgiven
him. Scudero was generally considered a little nuts, so St. Clair
could not totally ignore his threats. Now Kuharich wanted him to
be as rough on offense. St. Clair wasn't stupid; the more he blocked
downfield, the fewer passes were likely to be thrown to him.

Everyone on the team played both ways, offensively and
defensively, but it was Kuharich's genius to identify a player's
strengths and weaknesses and to get the most out of him. He
was learning at the same time as his players, imparting his
knowledge and that of his coaches in teaching his new passing

formations. Ralph Thomas was a great pass rusher and so quick that he could seal off any play that attempted to sweep outside. So on defense, he was first-string left end. At that position, which required much running and quick, explosive speed, Kuharich couldn't expect him to be running downfield on offense as well, so he played behind St. Clair as second-string right end. He still got his offensive snaps, just not very many. When he did go in on offense, Kuharich had special plays for him. Only seven of the starters played first-string both ways, and even they had been given the strongest players as their back-ups. Toler, who just never seemed to tire, St. Clair, Marchetti, Stephens, Brown, Matson, and Scudero were the ones Kuharich counted on to go both ways. It was not lost on the coaches or even on me that these were probably, except for Thomas, the most gifted players on the squad. If you looked deeper into the coaches' reasoning, you became aware that except for Scudero, they were very large men. Brown was large as a quarterback at 6'2" and fast enough to be a running threat. On defense, playing right corner, he was huge for that position. Even Scudero, playing safety at a hundred and sixty-five and 5' 7", had a tremendous advantage. He was very quick, and playing alongside Matson at free safety in the offensive backfield, he was not expending as much energy as if he were the featured back. Kuharich believed that Kerr's assessment of Scudero's mental state was not that far off the mark. Scudero would hit a receiver or a running back who got through the line with a violence that belied his weight and stature. He was just a little nuts.

As the second week of camp wore on, Kuharich started pulling individual players aside for sessions with the coaches. He chose offensive and defensive captains in Brown and Toler. Toler was somewhat of a surprise to his staff in that this was the first year he had actually played under a system. Kuharich still shouted in his high-pitched voice and used words inappropriately in his speeches. He still mixed his metaphors, but even though their work load hadn't diminished, the players could sense that he approved of their performance.

There were even some events that second week that lightened the mood. Just before noon on Tuesday, a day after Quart had been sent home, with a half-hour of hard scrimmage left in the morning session, a convertible filled with five young girls pulled up in the parking lot adjacent to the field. The girls got out and moved to the sidelines opposite, where Ed Brown was taking snaps and launching missiles down field to Merrill Peacock and Bob St. Clair. They started cheering and clapping with every reception, Brown and the receivers waving as they finished the route. After the third catch, Kuharich had had enough; the players were paying more attention to the girls than to the drill. Kuharich yelled at Scrap Iron to clear the girls out, which he did by jogging over and yelling at them that this was a private work-out and they must leave. Scrap Iron was not a pretty man; in fact, he was kind of scary. The girls piled into the car and took off, only to reappear on the other side of the field a few minutes later, again opposite Brown, who was smiling and telling the receivers to go deep. That was it for Kuharich. The megaphone went up and the girls were greeted with a series of commands that would have frightened the players if they had been directed at them. The girls simply giggled as Scrap Iron ran in slow motion across the field, waving his hands and shouting at them himself. Watching the trainer run, and hearing the volume of Kuharich's voice rise, the squad stopped the drills, standing still and holding their laughter with only a little success.

Kuharich also allowed the players that second week to take off their helmets on the drills and no-contact work outs. They still had to wear them during scrimmages and when in the Pit, but at other times they could go bare-headed or even wear their straw hats.

That afternoon Scudero had just run a pass route, catching the perfect spiral from Brown. The whistle blew and Kuharich called for a contact scrimmage. Scooter, the name by which the team had started to call Scudero, ran to the sideline where the helmets were discarded and grabbed Colombini's by mistake. He put it on his head. The helmet was huge, Scudero's head small. He yelled for everyone to look at him and then spun the helmet around so the face opening was in the back, walking backward with his hands reversed. Getting the laughs he wanted, he took it off and read that it was Colombini's helmet.

"Christ, what a head you have, a real Grande Casaba!"

As they came to the sideline to grab their own helmets, the players took up the chant, "Grande Casaba," as Colombini came up and ripped his helmet away from Scudero. His head was large, and he had just picked up a nickname of his own, "Casaba"—one even the coaches would adopt over the next two years.

On Friday, Kuharich ran morning practice late, getting everyone back to the hotel at one in the afternoon. They showered and had lunch, then packed up their gear and straw hats and got back on the bus. I took a seat next to Brad Lynn that was probably reserved for one of the other coaches. I wanted the opportunity to talk to him more about his recruiting of some of the players, to get more stories. We had been out of touch, isolated for the two weeks in Corning. The coaches would find out that isolation didn't mean much to me as far as doing my job. Every evening I would write a story about something that had happened, or about one of our players or coaches, and send it off to the papers in the city. I had to make sure that all of them got something so it wouldn't look like I played favorites. It was a little more work, but there were nights I wrote three completely different stories about the same incident, but from different perspectives. The coaches would arrive to the Monday *San Francisco Chronicle* featuring a spread in the Green section by Will Connolly about the training camp. It was all there: the temperature, the olives, the straw hats, and most of all the loss of weight the players had experienced: Colombini's fifteen pounds the first week, Stanfel's eighteen, St. Clair, who couldn't afford to lose much on his spare frame, losing twelve pounds, even Ed Brown now using the fifth hole on his belt when he had been using the second when they'd gotten on the bus to travel to Corning—it was all chronicled, along with Coach Kuharich's explanation that no muscle tissue was lost, only water weight through the pores.

I had begun my quest to get the USF football team noticed.

CHAPTER TEN

NFL Offices

We had gone up to Corning over the Bay Bridge, but once we got to Vallejo on the trip south, we headed west over Highway 37 to Marin County and across the Golden Gate Bridge. It was still hot going through San Rafael and Mill Valley, but as we went through the new Waldo Tunnel and approached the bridge, the temperature dropped sharply and we could see a solid bank of fog reaching across the bridge, showing only the very top of its tower abutments. The fog flowed through the Golden Gate like a two-headed silver serpent as it separated and humped over Alcatraz Island and on into Berkeley, the home of the University of California.

The cooling effect of the fog hit while we were still a mile away and coming down onto the bridge approach. Without anyone being conscious of starting it, the players began cheering and clapping. I glanced over at Kuharich and saw him smile as he was nudged by Coach Kerr to his outside.

The Golden Gate Bridge, connecting the northwestern corner of San Francisco to Marin County, is an icon. It is so much a symbol of San Francisco that it has become part of the identity of the city. Show anyone in the world its picture and they will respond, "That's San Francisco." Because of its name, most tourists expect the bridge to be painted gold instead of the red lead-brick color of the anti-rust paint that covers it from end to end. The name Golden Gate had been given to the opening to the Bay long before the bridge was even proposed. It was what the miners and sailing vessels named it during the Gold Rush of 1849.

The bridge opened on May 27, 1937, making it younger than the players on the team. The prospect of a bridge connecting the two sides of the Bay had been proposed as early as 1869, but it began to be talked about in earnest in 1916 by the city engineer, Michael O'Shaughnessy, who had been hired in 1912 after laying out the towns of Mill Valley and Sausalito, the two towns directly north of the Gate. O'Shaughnessy was a visionary during his tenure as Chief City Engineer and an unabashed advocate of all things that would benefit the city's residents. He designed the streetcar system, including the tunnels, and proposed the Hetch Hetchy water project, designing the hundreds of miles of underground water tunnels that brought the water to San Francisco from the main dam in Yosemite. An Irishman born in Limerick, he had graduated from the University College in Cork. Cork, like San Francisco, is situated on a land mass surrounded by bays and inlets with many bridges providing access to the surrounding islands and countryside.

In 1915 San Francisco had hosted a World's Fair. One of the attractions was an amusement ride utilizing a counter-weighted system that took a hundred people over two hundred feet in the air, high enough to view the Golden Gate, the narrow entry to the San Francisco Bay. The ride was designed by a bridge builder out of Chicago named Joseph Strauss.

O'Shaughnessy questioned several engineers as to the possibility of creating a link between the land masses, now served only by ferries. The estimated cost for most of the proposals was $100 million. Strauss's estimate was $25 to $30 million, and he was awarded the contract. It was not a smooth process, however.

First, Strauss's initial design was a hybrid, half suspension bridge and half trestle. It was described as "butt ugly" by critics, and he subsequently submitted, with the help of several other engineers, another plan for the suspension bridge that was finally built with a main span of 5,000 feet between towers. It was over twice as long as any suspension bridge at the time. For the bridge to be built, first funding had to be obtained, and it was not easy. Then the Great Depression hit in 1929, and it was not until 1932 that a bond measure was placed in front of the voters. It looked as if the bond would fail until Bank of America's president, A.P. Giannini, financed over $6 million of the bond with the sole motivation of increasing the local economy, which made Giannini millions in return.

The construction was an engineering feat unknown to the world at the time. A trestle was extended from the north and south into the bay. Strauss had to modify the southern San Francisco construction and road approach to preserve Fort Point, a Civil War fort, at the entrance to the bay. From these platforms, divers went down 90 feet on each side of the entrance to blast rock and provide solid abutments, which would support the towers that would rise 400 feet into the air above them. A San Francisco firm invented a machine that would climb a thin cable from the shore to the top of the tower, then down and up to the other tower and onto the other side. Each trip it made, it braided a thin cable into the one already strung. Back and forth it went like a mechanical spider between San Francisco and Marin County until the finished cable was the size of a manhole cover. Smaller cables were then dropped from the west and east cables down and around the roadway that was slowly extending out to the center of the span. The final cable would stretch over 7,650 feet in length. It was dangerous work, but until four months prior to the bridge's opening, there was only one fatality. Nineteen men had fallen, only to be caught by safety nets. These lucky individuals started a club named the "Halfway to Hell Club." In February, just a few months before the May opening, a scaffold broke loose, tearing through the netting and causing the deaths of ten workers.

The bridge opened to 200,000 people allowed to walk across the bridge's automobile lanes. The next day FDR officially opened the bridge to automobile traffic by telegram from the White House.

Joseph Strauss is generally credited with the bridge's creation, and he was indeed the project's chief engineer, as well as being extremely active politically both in San Francisco and the North Bay during the years when permits and financing were almost as difficult as construction. Strauss stood all of five feet tall. His ego, though, made up for his lack of stature. It was notable to anyone visiting him at the house he built to live in during the building of the bridge. The doorways were just six feet high and many of them used rounded arches so that the sides were even lower. The house was built some 40 feet above the water of the bay on Belvedere Island in Marin County. It had a full-on view of the entrance to the bay where the bridge—his bridge—was being built.

Strauss's original bridge design had been rejected; its only redeeming feature was that the price tag was only $17 million. The eventual design was suggested by one of his assistant engineers, and most of the engineering formulas and mathematics were done by another. At completion, the Bridge district that oversaw the construction refused to pay for a statue, partly because Strauss's ego had alienated so many of the directors and partly because he had discredited so many of his assistant engineers in his history of the bridge's construction. Strauss's widow eventually funded the bronze statue that sits on the south end of the bridge approach, above Fort Point.

For the players on the bus, the bridge had always been there. The fog they often blamed for the chill on campus was now welcomed by all. Traveling the 1.7 miles across the bridge's span meant that they were home again. If they needed more reassurance, as they pulled up to the campus on the hill, the fog ended and a much cooler sun shone down upon them.

Riding next to Coach Lynn had been most productive. He had a good sense of humor and was friendly and open. It was plain to see why he was such a good recruiter. I think he embellished a few of the stories he told me about recruiting some of the kids, but after getting to know the players at Camp Kuharich, and after what I had seen them do, I concluded that he had not had to stretch the truth very much.

Later, when I sat down and talked with Joe Scudero, he confirmed a part of Lynn's account and added a whole new angle as well. Scudero had grown up in San Francisco's Ingleside District. Before the war, San Francisco was rigidly divided by ethnic group. As an Italian, Scudero should have been in North Beach or the Marina, but instead he was in an area filled with Irish, who spilled over from South of Market, and with Latinos from the Mission District. The working-class families were mostly looking for work in the aftermath of the Great Depression and World War II. The kids ran rough and often in gangs. By the time Scudero was seventeen, he had an impressive rap sheet, mostly for fighting. A lot of the fights were with older, bigger kids, and the police who were often called in to clean up the mess at first thought Little Joe was being targeted because of his size. Then came the two-on-one attacks, and still little Joe was getting the best of them. At some point the police came to realize that Scudero was probably looking for the fights rather than running from them. One report was particularly telling. I had a few hours off one Monday afternoon and found that one of the arrests had been written down in a report by Sergeant Walsh at the Mission Police station. Father Feeley told me about it and phoned the officer, who let me see the file.

This was Scudero's account: "These four guys chased me home one day. I was faster than they were, so there was no danger, but my father was home and saw what happened. I didn't tell him that I had beaten the crap out of each of the guys over the last month and that they had ganged together to teach me a lesson. Dad went downstairs and came back with a baseball bat. 'Use it if they try that again, or else they will own you. Just don't hit them in the head.'

"The next day I went to school with the bat, and sure enough, the four guys were waiting for me on the way home. When we were far enough from school that we wouldn't be seen, I turned a corner and waited for them. The word went out. 'Don't mess with Scudero. He's crazy!' I didn't really have much trouble after that."

During his senior year, Brad Lynn had watched Scudero in three games, including the one in which St. Clair had almost decapitated him. He was the best high school back Lynn watched that year, the best period except for Ollie Matson, who was a couple years older and playing for the San Francisco City Junior College team. Scudero was wobbly as he went off the field after the St. Clair hit, but after just one series he was back in the game, as quick and punishing as ever. Lynn watched him the whole second half. He was not as effective as in the first half. At first he thought it was because of the hit, but he soon realized Scudero was often leaving his assignment to try and put one over on St. Clair, who was almost twice his size. Later Lynn went to the sidelines to tell the players "good game" and saw Scudero with his helmet off. His entire right eye was puffed shut and that side of his face was already turning into a spectacular purple bruise.

The first day he could legally contact high school seniors, Lynn knocked on the door of Scudero's house. He was dressed as usual in a coat and tie. Scudero's mother opened the door cautiously, mistaking Lynn in his tie for a juvenile officer.

"Joey is at the police station. Some boys were picking on him again." She started to close the door on Lynn, who managed to get in a few words before the door slammed.

"I'm Coach Lynn from the University of San Francisco."

The door stopped.

"The University of San Francisco? I think Father Feeley is with him. He's such a nice man. He watches out for Joey."

"Which police station?" asked Lynn.

Lynn found Scudero sitting on a bench in the hallway of the Mission Police Station, holding an ice pack to his face. He was about to approach the boy when a voice called out his name. He turned and saw Father Feeley, a Jesuit from USF, emerging from one of the doors that opened into the hallway.

"What are you doing here?" asked the priest.

"I was at this young man's house to talk to him about coming to the university to play football for Coach Kuharich."

Scudero looked up, then slumped back down, pondering his self-imposed bad luck at being found in this circumstance.

Father Feeley was followed out of the doorway by a police sergeant, who moved to Scudero, pulling the ice pack from his already coloring right eye.

"Let me guess, Joseph—you didn't start this one either?"

Scudero answered with a sheepish shrug.

"Did you hear what Coach Lynn just said? I hope you haven't messed this up."

"Sergeant Walsh," said Feeley. "Are you going to press charges here?"

"I might if he shows up here again. It's the third time this year. This time we just brought him in to protect the two kids he was fighting with. They ran when the patrolman showed up."

"Coach Lynn and I can take him home then?"

"Kid," the sergeant said, pointing his finger at Scudero's chest. "You're a hell of a player, but you're more lucky than good.

You're lucky I'd do anything for USF. But from now on, stay the hell out of my precinct, or it's Juvie for you."

Outside, they climbed into Lynn's car. Father Feeley had taken the bus when Sergeant Walsh phoned him, knowing that he was Scudero's confessor, something that Lynn did not know.

As the door closed, Lynn looked over the seat with a grin and asked, "Do you always lead with your right eye? Isn't that the same one St. Clair closed a couple of months ago?"

"That cheap shot. I'll get even with that chump."

"I hope not. He's coming to USF. You'll be teammates. Now let's go to USF and talk about how we can make that happen."

CHAPTER ELEVEN

To be home implies a comfortable room, a soft bed, maybe a view, and a mother to look over most of one's needs, especially laundry. As the players debarked the bus from Corning, this was not what greeted them. Many lived in San Francisco; some were even married. These took streetcars and buses home, but the majority filtered into the university housing, called the barracks—and barracks they were. Left over from World War II when USF had provided education for officers and other servicemen on their way to the Pacific theater, the buildings were nothing more than a series of Quonset huts, some arranged in a closed rectangle. They housed up to fifty students apiece. They were only single-walled, offering no insulation. The heater was centrally located, its warmth barely reaching the far ends. The floors were at least covered with linoleum, which always seemed to be ten degrees colder than the air temperature. Each dormitory had a prefect, usually a grad student or an upperclassman, who was supposed to keep order. One was even staffed by a Jesuit. The football team was housed almost exclusively in a single barrack.

The players filed into the building, staking out their beds, not at the end and not too close to the heat. There was a small communal area where they could play cards, but no kitchen. Cooking was forbidden in the Quonsets because of the danger from fire. The prefect responsible for the freshman football players' dorm was a young graduate student named John Lo Schiavo.

He was a brilliant student with a soft-spoken way about him and a personality that made him universally liked. He was destined to become a Jesuit, but at this time he was still a student. After his ordination, he became Dean of Men in the early sixties, then University President and Regent—one of the most universally beloved of all priests and administrators.

The upper-class football players were brutal to their prefects, running off two with their antics. It fell on Lo Schiavo to double up his duty, which he did by overlooking many of the less oner-ous offenses of the upper-classmen, such as screaming during games of Hearts and the occasional cooking of extra food in the dorm late at night, since the athletes were always hungry; many a time, the food and electric grill were handed outside through the window as the prefect entered at the other end of the building.

The older players were men both in age and experience. Some, such as Marchetti, had fought in the war. Some were in their mid-twenties and from big cities. There were a few play-ers who were quiet and studious; Burl Toler and Ralph Thomas were in that group, a stark contrast to the group from Chicago, which was particularly boisterous, having grown up in that city during and after Prohibition. The locals—Marchetti, St. Clair, Joe Scudero, Ed Brown, Roy Barni, and Tringali—were not to be outdone, especially Tringali. They did more than hold their own. Tringali, having grown up in North Beach, knew all the best places in town to get into trouble. The players used the close confines of their less-than-ideal quarters to meld into a cohesive unit that fall of 1950.

Kuharich's office and those of his staff were also located in the barracks. On the second day back from Corning, he called a coaches' meeting. I was invited.

"We have a great opportunity this year, gentlemen. You have seen our players over the last two weeks. Most of them just have raw talent. They have little sense of how to play football, particularly as a team. That is our challenge this year. To win, of course, but more to teach the players fundamentals. Every good team must have a star. I think we may have as many as five who could achieve that level.

"Brad, there are four players on the freshman squad we will desperately need next year to fill the graduation spots. The fortunate thing is that the players we will lose this year are not the heart of the team. In fact, I think that if freshmen could have played last year, two or three of them would have started—St. Clair, for sure. It will be the same this year. It is your job to coach them in the same system they will see with the varsity.

"The rest of us have to break these wild stallions and coach them to play as a unit. Coach Kerr, I want you to pay particular attention to Toler, Marchetti, and St. Clair. Toler might be our best athlete, but he has only had a year and a half of football. It's the same with Marchetti. St. Clair is just stubborn, with an ego as big as his body. He will fight you at every turn. He has developed some bad techniques that he gets away with because of his size. Defensive left end is where I see him, with Marchetti and Toler on the quarterback's blind side. Leave him as right offensive end. At his size, I don't see how Brown can miss him on pass routes.

"The team we inherited two years ago was not very good. Last year, our 7 – 3 record showed promise, but the record was better than we were. What it really did was help our recruiting efforts. Brad and Scrap Iron got a lot of the players I'm talking about because we could show that promise. We must keep that going, and it will not be easy. This year's schedule has one more game and is significantly harder, with both Cal and Stanford on the schedule. There are two quarterbacks, Le Baron and Klosterman, on the schedule who are cinch professionals. We need to keep the wins coming and still develop our raw talent into a cohesive unit."

"Boss," said Coach Kerr as Kuharich finished his remarks, which was like a reading of the Bill of Rights. "I think we have the players to win now, this year."

"Win, yes, but not excel. Perhaps by the end of the year, but they are still too inexperienced. Last year we saw what Matson could do at the junior college level. We need to devise blocking schemes to let him use that speed and power. Joe Scudero is the perfect complement to Matson, but a different blocking scheme will be needed for his style out of the same formation. Managed correctly, he could be a star as well. At quarterback, Brown took a number of snaps from Jim Ryan and Sweeters last year. Does anyone disagree that Brown has the bigger upside? We must integrate him into the passing game. Peacock is proving to be a very worthy pass catcher. We need to have passing plays for that skill, more so than in the past. You know what I think about the ground game. It is the foundation for the success of any passing game."

"So win this year, but what we are actually doing is developing players for next year, 1951," said Brad Lynn.

"Don't misunderstand me," said Kuharich. "We try to win every game while developing the team and our playbook for next year, when we'll be much better, both as players and coaches."

It would be impossible to overstate the effect the 1950 season had on the following year's team. Their record for the year was 7 wins and 4 losses. The players Kuharich had red-flagged learned, became stronger and more skilled, and began playing to one another's strengths. But three games had a direct effect on what was to transpire the following year.

The first game in 1951 was played in Kezar Stadium under the lights against the University of Tulsa Golden Hurricane. The Dons won 23–14 and played a vicious hitting game, in part due to the players coming of age and in part motivated by a 0–10 loss to the same team that had occurred the year before. I had not traveled with the team in 1950 and was unaware of the whole story. I knew that Kuharich was livid about the southern officiating that had targeted Matson and Toler, calling back scores for nonexistent fouls and allowing the Tulsa players to pile on Matson long after the whistle. In that game, the Dons had led in almost every category except for passing yards and the final score. That would have been enough to want to exact revenge, but it was the off-the-field events that truly whetted the players' appetites to dominate the team from Oklahoma.

I had noticed the intensity of practice, not from the coaches or Kuharich but from the players themselves. It could only be described as pure nastiness. Scrap Iron used more tape and dirt rubs that week than he had the whole pre-season. I pulled Bill Henneberry aside and asked him what was up. I sensed a story when Bill hesitated, looking down at the ground. Bill was one of the most honest people I had ever met. I mean, he wouldn't even exaggerate to improve a story! After a few hems and haws, while I smiled and looked at him expectantly, he told me a story about the night before the previous year's game in Tulsa.

Bill was with seven of the players, cooling off in an old downtown Tulsa tavern with a poorly lit sign: Johnny Boy's Icehouse. The table looked like a landfill of empty lemonade glasses, potato chips, and pretzels, with a few empty beer glasses scattered among them. A handful of locals and two waitresses listened to a jukebox along the back wall.

Marchetti asked St. Clair, "What the hell is a Golden Hurricane?" That was the University of Tulsa's mascot.

Joe Scudero, without waiting for St. Clair to answer, said, "It's a big puff of wind, kind of like a burp or a fart. Kind of like you, St. Clair."

The locals who overheard this were not pleased, but neither Scudero nor Marchetti seemed to notice.

"Where's Tringali? I like his music better than what's on the juke," replied St. Clair, hiding his annoyance.

The rest lifted their glasses in agreement with the big man.

"Somebody see if there's anything good on that thing."

Scudero walked over to the jukebox and threw a hip into it, causing the needle to skip across the record. Every eye in the bar turned to the rear as Scudero pulled out a dime and slid it into the slot, punching the button for "Goodnight Irene." The song began as Scudero returned to the table, staring down the other patrons as they glared at him.

Bob St. Clair nudged Marchetti. "Are you listening to those two old farts at the bar?" He motioned toward two locals talking loudly with their backs to the table only four feet away. The two men were in a heated discussion about their own playing days, oblivious to the other customers and evidently hard of hearing, as they were almost shouting at each other. The lineup of empties in front of them might have influenced the content of their conversation as well as its volume.

"These young punks keep adding all kinds of protective gear. It's hardly a man's game anymore."

"They're all pussies. They wouldn't have lasted in our time."

"I know what you mean. Hell, after all the time I spent in the trenches during the Great War, I could play football naked."

"My nephew, a real wise-ass, had the nerve to ask me if I could play in this era. I told him the question really was, could these college candy asses play with us?"

A waitress delivered a new bottle to each of the old men, clearing off the bar in front of them. The one on the left took a swig of his beer and leaned over the bar, spanking the woman on her rear. The waitress was unfazed but turned and gave the old man the stink eye. She started to say something but was distracted by the entry door opening and Tringali, Toler, Brown, and Matson stepping inside.

The Dons at the table welcomed their teammates enthusi-
astically, but the rest of the patrons, including the two old men,
reacted as if aliens from outer space had just entered the bar.
Tringali led the new group to the bar, figuring he would shorten
the time getting something cool in their hands, as Marchetti
yelled, "Bartender, drinks for my teammates."

The bartender took the order and handed Tringali a beer and
Brown a lemonade, ignoring Matson and Toler.

Marchetti got up from the table and approached the bar. "I
said drinks for *all* my teammates."

"I'm good, big guy," said Toler.

"Lemonade, please," said Matson, oblivious to the situation.

Marchetti arrived at the bar as Tringali fingered his bottle
and Brown put a quarterback's grip on the now-empty glass.

The two old guys smiled, knowing what was about to take
place. Henneberry, who had been nursing his cherry Coke, could
sense there was going to be trouble. He had not grown up a delin-
quent like Scudero or St. Clair, roaming his neighborhood looking for fights. He thought he had better try to get the team out
of there. He started toward the bar, but he wasn't quick enough.

"Not here. We serve whites only."

The two old farts' smiles grew.

The bartender started to bend over, reaching under the counter and grasping a shotgun. Marchetti didn't flinch a millimeter.
Instead he leaned toward the danger, knocking the shotgun away
with a meaty left hand. The bartender moved back against the
row of bottles at his back.

All the players were on their feet now, backing Marchetti.

"Pal," said Marchetti, reaching out and grabbing the bartender by his shirtfront. "I got two truisms for ya. One: no one
remembers weak men. Two: I ran into plenty of creeps like you
during the war and they didn't scare me either. I think you were
about to pour a couple of lemonades."

The room grew deathly silent. The jukebox stopped playing, then reloaded "Goodnight Irene." The two old farts were the only ones smiling.

Marchetti's hand moved with superhuman quickness as he pulled the bartender over the bar so close their noses nearly touched.

Henneberry watched as Burl Toler moved to his friend, putting his arm around Gino's shoulder. "Big guy! I thought I told you I don't drink. Let's go."

Seeing the opportunity, Henneberry pulled himself together and moved quickly to Marchetti's other shoulder. "What's the point, Gino? You can crush this guy like a grape, but it might ruin the whole season. Let him go … gentle … easy … the party's over." Brown took Henneberry's lead and the two quarterbacks turned to the Dons who were still crowded around the bar. "I think we're done here, gentlemen. Let's get back to the hotel before Coach begins to wonder." Brown put a handful of bills on the bar and said to the bartender, "This should cover any damage."

The team, at first slowly, then with a purpose, got up and left the bar, keeping an eye on Gino, who still had the bartender pulled half over the bar. The gigantic St. Clair moved to Marchetti's side and the two left together, both watching the bartender as they did so.

"Maybe the game hasn't gone to shit after all," said the first old man in a chastened tone. His companion nodded his agreement.

The hotel was a short two blocks away from Johnny Boy's Icehouse. Marchetti and the others entered, finding the rest of the team already stuffing themselves in the dining area. As the group noisily took up seats, Toler and Matson remained at the entrance as if frozen, halted by a small sign screwed to the wall to the right of the door. The others, obviously hungry, were already eating dinner rolls while they waited for more meat and potatoes to be sent by the kitchen.

Coach Kerr noticed the two players and got up and walked toward them, speaking softly to Toler, who tapped Matson and nodded his head toward the hotel lobby.

Scudero turned to Colombini, motioning to the two departing players. "What's up? Aren't they hungry? We got a game tomorrow."

Gino overheard Scudero. "Is this a whites-only hotel? Son of a … After the shit we dealt with tonight."

Scudero and Colombini got up, quickly followed by Tringali. They rushed out after Matson, Toler, and Kerr, who were about to get into a car parked outside the hotel.

"Hold on. We're coming too."

"We're going to a Black hotel, guys."

"Yeah, and that's where we're going too. We can't have you two sleeping in late tomorrow. Wait a minute while we get our bags," said Scudero as he grabbed the arms of the other two and sprinted back into the building.

Coach Bud Kerr didn't say anything; he just smiled and slowly edged himself into the driver's seat.

CHAPTER TWELVE

Despite defeating Tulsa in the first game of the year, Kuharich was not a happy man. It was his opinion that the overwhelming of the Golden Hurricane was a result of the one-on-one fury shown by most of his players. The victory lacked the precision required by a squad working as one. There was more to it than just losing to the Tulsa team the previous year; revenge would be a normal motive in an individual or a team, but the fury and viciousness of the singular battles showed more than that basic instinct. He had watched Marchetti three times pound an offensive blocker into the turf, pummeling him into the ground rather than breaking contact and following the flow of the play.

Without naming my source, I had told Kuharich what I had learned about some of the off-field confrontations while the team was in Oklahoma the previous year. As a coach, he could understand the need to stick up for one's teammates, but he believed it shouldn't be done at the expense of team play. Kuharich was worried about the second game of the year against Stanford, down on the Farm. It would be perhaps the hardest of all the eleven games they would play in the most ambitious schedule a USF team had ever had. The Stanford team was big, well coached, and playing on its own turf.

The coach would be proven correct, as Stanford dominated the game 55 to 7. The Dons, as they had done in game one, took their roles as individual contests. Kuharich was not the only one to observe that tendency in the Tulsa game. Stanford had two scouts watching that night game under the lights at Kezar. Every time an individual acted singly, the Stanford team made them pay. When Marchetti left his assignment to inflict punishment on an individual offensive player, a second option was either a halfback run over his vacated position or a swing pass for a good gain just out of reach of the prostrate Don. The result was two-fold: a dramatic defeat on the scoreboard and a number of the Stanford first-stringers in question for their following game due to injury. Despite the score, the Stanford coaching staff thought many of the USF players were playing dirty, and they wanted nothing to do with scheduling them in 1951.

Marchmont Schwartz, the Indians' head coach in 1950, was, like Kuharich, a two-time All-American at Notre Dame under Knute Rockne as a halfback. He had joined the Stanford coaching staff just before the war in 1940 and coached the Wow Boys, who went undefeated to the Rose Bowl, defeating Nebraska. He took what the scouts had told him about the Dons' previous games and with his knowledge of Notre Dame's coaching strategy, which he was sure Kuharich would use, he looked at game films and devised his game plan. His expertise in coaching the backfield allowed him to devise a dozen passing plays which, if his offensive line could allow time for his quarterback to identify a secondary receiver, would be effective against the Dons' aggressive defense. Stanford's game plan, if executed correctly, would take advantage of some huge holes, particularly on the right side, as, after watching films of Toler and Marchetti, he scrupulously avoided their side of the field. It worked perfectly, but he underestimated the price that his starting players would pay. Due to the physical nature of the USF game, a large number of Stanford players were injured and less effective for many of the following weeks. Schwartz and Stanford, after a good start that season, posted a disappointing 5–3–2 mark, and he resigned following the season. Chuck Taylor, an All-American lineman on the famous Wow Boys team, took over Stanford in 1951. Schwartz's last piece of advice to Taylor upon leaving was, "Don't schedule the team from USF. They cost me the job." Taylor took the advice to heart and despite numerous pleas from the Dons' coaching staff, he refused to play them in 1951. It was a good decision for the new Indians coach, as his 1951 team rolled to nine straight wins before losing to archrival Cal in the "Big Game" and again to Indiana in the Rose Bowl.

The second 1950 game that would negatively affect the following season for the Dons was their contest against the strong University of California Bears. It was their ninth game of the season and it was played in Berkeley under torrential rains. The field was drenched by the time of kickoff, sloppy by the end of the first quarter, a muddy bog by the start of the second half, and then it got worse. The final score was 13 to 6, with the mighty, highly regarded Bears feeling lucky to get the win. Like most of the crowd that had stayed through the game, the reporters knew that USF had more than the statistical edge and thought the Dons had done enough to win the game, as did the Bears' legendary head coach, Pappy Waldorf. Like Chuck Taylor, he would deny the Dons a chance for redemption in 1951.

Throughout the season, Kuharich taught, coached, and chastised his individually talented players on both technique and the science of a well-designed play. Defensively, it was more difficult to get them to play together as a unit, because in an offensive play they had the advantage of knowing in advance what they were supposed to do and where to be on the field, while defense was more a matter of reaction to what the other squad was doing. It was his luck that the studious Burl Toler, playing his defensive tackle position, took on identifying the opposing team's plays at the line. Toler, with only two years of football experience, seemed to respond quickly to how the opponent was lining up, picking up on clues unknowingly revealed by the opposing linemen and their backfield. He also knew not only his own responsibilities but also those of every other member of the team behind him. Halfway through the schedule, Kuharich named him defensive captain, giving him responsibility for calling the defensive sets. Marchetti got it almost as fast as Toler, and the two of them made the right side of the defensive line almost impenetrable. Tringali, on the line with them, and Scudero and Matson playing behind them soon learned to trust Toler's defensive calls. On the left side, St. Clair, because of his size and athletic ability, was able to block or discourage many quarterback passes, even if he was not in the place he was supposed to be in the defensive scheme.

Spring and early summer progressed with a feeling of plea-surable anticipation among the members of the coaching staff as to the readiness of the squad, and only one area of concern. The team schedule was missing two games. Stanford and Cal had emphatically refused to put USF on their schedule. What was worse, they had spread the word to both UCLA and USC. Kuharich even called Notre Dame, hoping someone might have cancelled but knowing that the Fighting Irish set their sched-ule up three years in advance. In the end, Kuharich had to settle for playing San Jose State twice in the same season, two service teams in Camp Pendleton, and the San Diego Navy. Those last two teams were more than they might have seemed on paper. It was the beginning of the Korean War. The draft was in prog-ress, and many of the players on both squads were college All-Americans or top-rated professional athletes now in the service, assigned to large bases with the pride of their base and branch of service behind them.

Kuharich, on the advice of Bud Kerr, used one ploy during the spring which worked quite effectively. He let it be known that they would probably be returning to Corning for training camp. In reality, he had been asked by Father Dunne to curtail that expense and develop plans to hold pre-season camp on the baseball field. There would be no 110-degree days, no shade from a single telephone pole, no Pit to be allowed to be scuffed out of the field surface by players trying their best to outmuscle each other, and to the relief of most, no olives. The result of his small deception was that the team showed up in their best physical shape ever at the start of camp. Not a single one wanted to go to Corning as they had the previous year without being in the best possible condition. It was what Kuharich had hoped for, as he felt that he had the measure of his team and the individual players. He planned more of a teaching clinic than the brutal camp of the year before. There were still miles of running through Golden Gate Park and thousands of push-ups and sit-ups, but the time allowed for camp was more like for a professional team, with refinement of techniques and the full installation of Ed Brown as quarterback. It allowed for and complemented the necessary increase of the playbook with the addition of a strong mix of passing plays.

I had not been idle during the summer. Realizing that many of the players would remain home either in San Francisco or near enough for me to contact them, I spent many days fleshing out my biographies of the individual players, learning their backgrounds, their off-field personalities, and their aspirations. If the coaches were looking forward to the '51 season, so was I. The better I knew the squad, the more chance for me to work magic with the publicity for the team. By season's start I had a stack of human interest stories tied to the team, individuals, and coaches ready to give to the reporters once the season began. When I wasn't talking to the players, I was roaming the sports desks of the *San Francisco Chronicle*, the *San Francisco Examiner*, and the *San Francisco Call Bulletin*, cementing relations with the scribes, Curley Grieve, Walt Daley, Bill Anderson, and Dick Toner.

One interview in particular that summer made me realize that this special football team Kuharich kept extolling was so because of the exceptional individuals it contained. Burl Toler was the perfect example. I found that many summer evenings, Burl would be on campus, in the library, studying from books that would be used the following semester.

I found the linebacker one evening studying at a large table in the nearly empty library and asked if I could have some of his time. Toler took off his reading glasses and closed the book he was studying. His voice was soft and polite, unexpected coming from a man of his size and clashing with the ferocity he displayed on the gridiron. The response was typical. "Sure, Pete. What can I do for you?"

I wanted to know how Burl, a kid from Tennessee, had somehow found his way to San Francisco and been talked into playing football at a junior college program when he had zero experience in the game. His enrolling at USF, I knew from talking with Coach Lynn, was the result of the coaches' recruitment of Ollie Matson: they had attended City College games and been impressed by Toler's play as an added benefit to watching Matson. Toler's choosing science as a subject at USF when most of the team was studying much easier majors was also of interest but not surprising given the young man's intelligence. USF had started as mainly a science teaching institution in 1855, and the faculty ninety years later still demanded dedication to the subject and held students to very high standards.

Memphis, Tennessee was not a hotbed of higher education for intelligent young Black men in 1946 when Burl graduated from Manassas High School. It was just after the war had ended, and the west coast was benefiting from the population growth it had seen during the war years; the opportunity for both jobs and education was too great a pull to resist. So 1947 saw Burl's father, Arnold, and mother, Annie, move their family to San

Francisco, where Burl enrolled in San Francisco City College. It was destined that he meet Ollie Matson. Ollie convinced Burl to go out for the football team on the basis of it being fun, with the added perk of advertising himself to the plethora of co-eds who came to the games. It didn't hurt that the team was loaded with great athletes and would go undefeated that year, winning the Mythical Junior College National Championship. Despite never having played a sport in high school, Burl excelled both on the field and in the classroom and was awarded All-American status along with Matson. In his quiet way, Burl glossed over his qualifications and instead told me about his first meeting with Coach Kuharich. Coach Lynn had arranged an appointment to see the head coach, Burl related to me, admitting that he was scared to death of the man from the accounts of him he had read in the papers.

Burl had knocked on the door to Kuharich's office and been given gruff, high-pitched permission to enter. The coach was shuffling papers around on his desk. As he arranged them in a pile, it was easy to see that each one of them had a name printed in bold pen strokes with the initials of a position to the right. Burl thought the stack looked over an inch high and felt any confidence that had been instilled in him by the ever-positive Coach Lynn seep away.

Kuharich asked where he was from, and Toler said Tennessee, at which the coach grunted and commented that he was a long way from home. He shuffled through the papers and found one with TOLER – LB printed across the top, studying it as if it was the first time he had seen it. "Manassas High School—an all-Black school? Did they teach you that education was the key?" Toler had answered in the affirmative, using the word "sir" at the end.

"You have very good manners. Good grades, too," mused Kuharich. Toler's parents were the prime movers in this regard, but I later learned that Manassas had an official school code that would have answered Kuharich's questions of the man in front of him. Manassas's creed was almost perfect: "Young men are taught good character, leadership and social skills. They have to learn cultural features of how to be a good man. You will always display respect for authority; using good speech and language; responding to adults with a yes sir or a no sir; a yes ma'am or a no ma'am. We want to lead by good and positive examples; to respect males and females alike, the young and the old. Our students keep their dignity and self-esteem at a high level, knowing that they are representing not only themselves, but their schools, homes, families, and communities, because first impressions usually create lasting impressions."

"Undefeated at City last year, JC All-American. Not bad for a kid just introduced to the game. Tells me you got a natural gift. Is that true, Mr. Toler? Do you have a natural gift?" Kuharich looked hard at Toler sitting across the desk from him, scanning his face for any sign of weakness and wondering about Coach Lynn's judgment. He had often seen gifted athletes who relied on their athletic ability and didn't work hard to improve their skills. It was hard for Kuharich to determine Toler's dedication or even his age from his appearance; he was a distinguished-looking youth, and with his wire-rimmed glasses, he looked more cut out for searching for rare books in the library than hunting down opponents on the gridiron, until you noticed the breadth of his shoulders and the muscles in his forearms extending beyond his white short-sleeved shirt. Burl's back was erect, and his eyes never left Kuharich's.

Kuharich made his decision, then spun the paper out of his hand onto his desk. The next words made Toler's heart jump. I could see the look of wonder on Toler's face as he recounted the meeting.

"If you come here, you will get an education. Education before football, but on my squad, not so very much before. If you apply yourself, you can excel in both. When you graduate, you will be equipped to be a success as a man in the world. And don't forget your Christian upbringing. You're not Catholic, and that should not matter to the Jesuits. Mr. Toler, I'm offering you a full scholarship to the University of San Francisco to play football."

Toler's response was typical of what Kuharich would see in him over the next two years. Without showing any excitement or concern about his future performance being up to the offer, Toler gave his two-word response. Standing up straight and looking the coach in the eye, he extended his hand. "I accept."

Then, when I thought Burl was finished telling of his recruitment visit, he reached over and put a massive hand on my forearm. "You know, Mr. Rozelle, like the coach said, I wasn't Catholic. I don't want you to misunderstand. I am Catholic now. I found something in the Jesuit teachings that was missing in my life. It meshed with the values we were taught in high school, but it held greater clarity. Ralph Thomas was my sponsor."

Ralph Thomas was much like Burl. He was quiet, studious, and very committed to his faith. He worked part-time as the switchboard operator at the Jesuit residence and knew all of the resident priests. He was thrilled when Burl took him aside and asked him to be his godfather and sponsor for his induction and baptism. Many of the players witnessed the ceremony that day.

Just prior to the fall session, I was walking across campus. If there was anything else I needed to know about this team that Coach Lynn and Scrap Iron had put together, or about the reason Burl Toler was so popular with his teammates, it would be put into perspective by what I saw that day.

Quarterback Ed Brown, Bob St. Clair, and Hal Sachs were lying on the grass above the football field, trying to catch some rays. Fog had prevailed over the campus the previous three days but had allowed the sun to make its appearance on the fourth. On the day of the incident, the sun was full blown on the campus, the fog barely covering the breakers on Ocean Beach three miles to the west. The temperature was nearing 74 degrees Fahrenheit, causing a wisp of steam to rise from the moisture-laden grass. Sachs, a natural beach boy despite his oversized athletic frame, would not miss a chance to maintain the saltwater tan he'd acquired during the summer.

I sat down on a nearby bench and extended my own profile to the sun. I had learned long ago to listen to discussions between the players rather than insert myself into the conversation by asking questions. Brown was saying that this camp was no Camp Kuharich like the one they had endured the previous year at Corning. The hours were just as long, but the drills and plays were much more intricate and interesting and were repeated at full speed, with more repetition and less full contact. His main complaint was that it kept him from doing his normal rounds, introducing himself to the "babes of the Bay," making sure they knew their man was back in town.

St. Clair agreed with Brown that the Barracuda was on a mission. Barracuda was the name the team had christened Kuharich with the previous spring because of the way his high-pitched voice would eviscerate any player who was giving anything less than his total effort or concentration to whatever task he was performing at the time. That was one thing that hadn't changed. The nickname Barracuda had stuck through the season that year, but all were careful that the coach never heard it. St. Clair was a frequent recipient of the coach's ire and didn't like being singled out. He accepted it in front of the coaches but complained constantly when he was with the other players. That day, as they lay together on the grass, I heard Brown call St. Clair a kiss-ass, and I had to hide a smile when St. Clair excused his behavior by saying the coach had great football smarts. The truth was, the more questions St. Clair asked, the less he was yelled at by the coach. I think it was because Kuharich thought the giant junior was finally showing interest in doing things the right way, rather than his way. Earlier in that day's lecture, Kuharich had tried to illustrate to the team that a group of dedicated men from a small college could prevail against great odds over foes with advantages both in numbers and resources. Kuharich had used the Spartan 300 as an example. St. Clair, not a great scholar in his own right, pointed out to the coach that he was sure the Spartans had conquered the Persians, not the Aversions, as the Coach had said.

Brown called him a kiss-ass again for correcting the coach when he had used the wrong word, causing Sachs to laugh out loud, as Toler came bouncing by, a load of books under his arm. Sachs got his laughter under control and invited Toler to join them in getting a tan. Burl looked at them with their shirts off and decided to join them. He came to the bench where I was sitting and removed his shirt, laying it on the bench before placing his books on top of it. He moved over to the others, his chest and back a slab of muscles, his sternocleidomastoid muscle taking a forty-five-degree angle from his ears toward his shoulder and giving him an 18-inch neck in the process. The other players moved apart and Burl took up a space between Sachs and Brown. He had hardly settled for ten seconds before he popped up like a Jack-in-the-box, pointing at his belly. His three teammates sat up, looking at him as he examined his stomach and chest.

"Oh my goodness," said Toler. "I'm turning pink. I gotta go see Scrap Iron and get some lotion before I bleach all the way white." Letting out his unique cackle, he grabbed his books, putting on his shirt one sleeve after the other, transferring the books while he did so, and sauntered off without another word.

Brown looked at Toler walking away, still cackling, and said, "I like that guy." The three players lay back down against the bench, chuckling to themselves at Toler's wit and the fact that Sachs had been upstaged. Toler headed toward the library, where another group of players, including Leo Madden, had gathered in the shade of a tree. As he approached, Madden separated from the group and moved to greet him.

I was too far away to hear what was said, but the look on both their faces caused me to make a mental note to find out later. Madden started to talk to Burl, who at first didn't stop. Then I saw Madden put a hand on Burl's arm, speaking earnestly to him. I got up and moved closer. They were still out of hearing of either group of players. It was obvious from the look on Madden's face that this was a serious conversation; I could tell that both from Madden's expression and from the way Burl had almost snapped to attention. The two talked for several minutes, and then Burl motioned one of the second group over to talk with them. My antenna went up full mast.

John Dwyer was an undersized stump of a lineman from Chicago. He had been openly critical of playing alongside Black men when he'd first arrived on campus and had again voiced his displeasure when both Matson and Toler had transferred in the year before. If there was any clique on the roster, it would be the group of players from Chicago; they tended to stick together, and Dwyer was recognized as one of their leaders. I had never seen any contact between Dwyer and either Matson or Toler in the previous year except on the field. With Madden standing by, Toler talked with Dwyer for several minutes before the Irishman turned back to the group he had left and began pointing and speaking with a sense of purpose. Madden and Toler watched him go, Madden shaking his head and clasping Toler on both shoulders before turning away, a smile replacing the frown he had worn just minutes before. I still could not catch anything more than the occasional word.

The next day I asked Coach James Ryan, the backfield coach, for the favor of talking to Madden during the first part of practice. Madden played backup left guard on offense behind Dwyer and backup left linebacker on defense behind Roy Giorgi. Despite his backup role, he showed leadership qualities and played with all his heart. I wanted to be able to talk to him away from the other players, hopefully in a relaxed atmosphere. I told Coach Ryan that it was no big deal, I just wanted to fill in some blanks in his biography, and it would only take a few minutes. Still, when he was called over and told to report to the publicity director, Madden looked around to see if any of the coaches were missing from the field. The players were never comfortable with meetings away from the rest of the team if there was any possibility the Barracuda would be involved.

I had talked with Madden several times, but never alone and always in casual conversation. I was not sure how to start this conversation, which my instincts told me would be anything but casual. I rose as Madden entered the office normally occupied by the assistant coaches, just outside of Kuharich's private workplace at the end of the Quonset hut, and offered him a Coke. Madden accepted the offer and settled uncomfortably into a seat, his pads making it a tight fit.

I had decided that the best approach was to be direct. I told Madden that I had seen Toler and later Dwyer talking with him the previous day and I wanted to help, if at all possible. Madden thought I knew more than I did and told me the whole story.

Madden had approached Toler as the captain of the defensive team. He had made up his mind that there was no answer to his predicament. He was convinced he would have to quit the team. He had explained to Toler that his father had died just two weeks previously after a prolonged illness, something all the players knew, and they had been mindful of Leo's grief. What Toler didn't know until Madden explained was that his mom was an invalid, incapable of taking care of herself. Leo had moved her to San Francisco after the funeral so that he could take care of her, but her needs were greater than he had realized. As he explained to Toler, "I just can't do it all—go to school, take care of her, play football, and maybe find a part-time job and make a little money." He explained that he was the first one in the family to go to college, and she desperately wanted him to graduate. He hadn't gone to Toler for a solution; he had looked for one and knew there wasn't one. He had gone to him as the team captain, wanting advice on the best way to tell the coaches, with the hope of keeping his scholarship until things got settled. What Toler offered took him completely by surprise.

Toler had not hesitated at all. He said that Leo was his teammate and they would find a way for him to continue. "You're one of us. The team will help you take care of your mom, and I'll help you with your studies. We're in two classes together. The rest of the guys will help as well, both with your mom and school. We'll get it done. Look, it's easy."

Toler had called over to the group of players, asking John Dwyer to join them. Burl, I found out later, was not sure how the Irish kid from Chicago would take to a Black man offering help to a white teammate with his mother. Toler did know that if he could enlist Dwyer, even Madden would understand that the whole team stood behind him. Toler had explained the problem and asked Dwyer to help organize the household assistance of Leo's mother while he organized help with the classroom and a part-time job. Toler had looked Dwyer directly in the eye, understanding that Dwyer had up to this point avoided both him and Ollie like the plague. Madden told me that Toler ended the conversation by saying to Dwyer, "John, this is a perfect way to prove what being a teammate really means on this squad, both to Leo here and to the coaches."

In just one evening they had worked out a schedule that would let the team split time with Madden's mother, negotiated with the professors to allow Leo to make up the occasional class or test as long as he performed well on his exams, and arranged for a part-time job with Bill Henneberry in the grocery store.

I knew that I would not use the story. It was too personal, a private circumstance that should be kept private for the sake of Leo Madden and his mother, but what it said about the team chemistry, and particularly Burl Toler's character, was hard to ignore. A week later in the weekly coaches' meeting, I retold the events to the entire staff. They had not heard what had been done by the team to help Madden, or of the kid's plight. Kuharich smiled.

CHAPTER THIRTEEN

There were disadvantages to having had a 7 and 4 season in 1950. First was the Corning training camp, which had instilled toughness in the individual players and brought them together, but San Francisco and its three major newspapers were 150 miles away. Even with my regular reports sent from Corning, the camp was not given the coverage that was extended to the football powerhouses Cal and Stanford. However, once the Dons came home to San Francisco, reporters in the city took joy in writing about the local team. The Dons were the only Division I team in the city. Dick Friendlich of the *Chronicle* went as far as to predict that an undefeated season was no mere dream.

As much good as the training camp had done, its rigors and the numerous second-hand articles that had been written about them resulted in high expectations. As the season progressed, the press put the other programs on notice. Through the spring and early summer of 1951, more articles were written, particularly about the four-star seniors who now had a full year under Kuharich's guidance and playbook schemes. It didn't help that several articles were written concerning the narrow loss to Cal. The result was that there was no way the Pac 8 would schedule the Dons. The football budget was such that the team could afford only one trip back east. Most of the games would by necessity be local or at least take place in California. There would be two games against San Jose State and two games against strong military teams loaded with ex-NFL players.

Dink Templeton of the *San Francisco Call Bulletin* voiced the outrage not only of Kuharich but of all San Francisco when he wrote, "The more I think about it, the greater shame it seems that the USF Dons have been frozen out of even a single conference game this season, while Santa Clara plays four conference opponents in its first five games. I can't believe that last year's story of USF's center throwing a punch in the Stanford game could result in a boycott. Nor that Cal would be insulted because Kuharich said the Dons would have walloped the Bears on a dry field—which they might just have done at that. But if they have anything other than that against USF, it's about time they came out with it openly. For though they might legitimately have been unable to find room for San Francisco, it is strange that all the other conference colleges found themselves in the same fix."

Kuharich had seen his coaching staff come together. He had seen his recruiting efforts do so as well; all pointed toward this 1951 season, in which his best players were seniors. They had lost Dick Stanfel to graduation and the Detroit Lions as their number one draft choice the previous year. Stanfel had been as much a coach to his two understudies as had the line coach, Bud Kerr. John Dwyer and Vince Tringali had learned much under Stanfel, both in scrimmages and skull sessions on technique, although Tringali still got more from his wild man approach than from being a technician.

As he watched the team develop both in practice and in games, Kuharich came to understand that he too would have to change. As I have mentioned, he had been born in South Bend, attended Notre Dame, played football under Knute Rockne, and become an All-American lineman and a professional football player. In all his experience, all his coaches' teaching, all his game plans, and all his playing days, he had relied on physical no-nonsense football. The running game was the power that won games. The ability to overcome an opponent with sheer brute force, to impose one's will on an adversary, was the essence of football. He despised easy touchdowns, those that came through the air, as was just now becoming popular in the professional game. He had watched the 49ers play at Kezar with Frankie Albert, the scanty little lefthander, hoisting passes over linemen who were intent on flattening him. The previous year the Cleveland Browns and the Los Angeles Rams had played in the NFL championship, which provided an aerial show never before seen in a championship game. As he watched those games, Kuharich came to realize that his guy, Ed Brown, was every bit as good a passer as any of those he had seen in the pros.

Kuharich recognized the trend, but he didn't like it. It wasn't the type of football he had learned, played, or coached. But two factors kept interfering with his justification for retaining the running game as the first and foremost offensive threat. The first was the way that both Fordham and Stanford had minimized Ollie Matson with a defense that keyed on running plays. They loaded the defensive line and put a spy player exclusively on Matson, especially for the formations that Kuharich had put in that featured Ollie's size and speed. Ollie's longest gain in the Fordham game was a forty-one-yard pass play.

The second was the development of Ed Brown as a passer. The year before he had used Brown primarily as a running back, sometimes replacing Matson due to a slight hamstring pull. As the season went on, Kuharich had experimented with letting Brown pass more. For this reason, and because they were playing catch-up in two of the last three games, Brown had established new USF records for passes thrown, completions, and touchdown passes. The Fordham game, coming in the middle of the season, was the clincher in Kuharich's decision to change his philosophy, at least with this group of athletes. Trailing 14 to

21 in the final minutes, and deep in their own field with almost ninety yards to go to score, Kuharich sent in two desperation pass plays. The crowd's eyes widened as both of Brown's passes were caught after traveling 60 yards through the air, although the first completion was negated by an offside penalty. The second pass was to Merrill Peacock, who caught the ball in mid-stride racing down the sideline and ran another 20 yards before being caught as the clock ran out.

It was not just Brown. It was the speedy Peacock, the massive St. Clair, the scatback Scudero, who was proving himself a fine receiver and running back, linked with a line of Marchetti, Hillig, Sachs, Stephens, and Toler, who could give Brown ample time to scout the field and rifle the pass. The personnel on the team dictated the type of offense Kuharich would run in the '51 season, and it would contain a good measure of passing plays. This did not prevent him from keeping the running game as the basis of his offense and using the passing game threat to stop opponents from loading the defensive line with linebackers and safeties.

A week of conditioning at the beginning of camp—which the players hardly needed, given the threats and disinformation about repeating Corning—led to drills that gave way to scrimmages that were more than spirited. For the first time since Kuharich had taken over the reins as head coach, he had a deep roster filled with true Division I players. It was no longer the first string against a group of players who were hoping to stop them. It was now the first string scrimmaging against those who wanted their jobs and were capable in many cases of replacing them. The result was that mistakes were costly for both sides, and instruction from the coaches went directly to the point. More was taught in less time, and the plays the team had learned at Corning and during the previous season now felt like second nature.

The camp was fun for both the coaches and the team. Only the baseball team had cause to complain, and they did complain about the field, which had been pristine the year before but this year was being chopped up by massive bodies wearing cleats and pushing each other around on the outfield grass. Still, playing against each other, facing the same opponent day after day, became both tiring and boring. Kuharich knew they were ready. A few minor fights had broken out as tempers flared with the repetition, players now thoroughly familiar with their opponents' numbers, moves, and tendencies. He thought he recognized the signs that the team was ready—more than ready—for their first game against San Jose State on September 21, 1951.

The season ahead would be a historic one, each game presenting new and different challenges to be overcome, but the finish of it would be a morality play far more lasting and important than a series of won athletic events. Winning became an expectation, a tradition that grew with each game.

CHAPTER FOURTEEN

Kezar Stadium – the home of the USF Dons football
team – 1940–1951

The late afternoon was sunny, the fog of the summer months now
gone, on Friday, October 21, 1951. On the USF campus, just over
half a mile from Kezar Stadium, the band was assembling, with
the sound of an occasional tuba burp or clarinet warble wafting
over the gathering of more than eight hundred students and faculty and twice the number of alumni and supporters of the team.
The campus beer and wine bar was doing brisk business as the
crowd assembled; it was convenient in that it was on campus, miti-
gating the need for fans to walk to the liquor store two blocks away
on Masonic and Fulton. It was clear, however, that many of the
alumni took advantage of the lower prices off campus and had six-
packs of Lucky Lager and Schlitz tucked under their arms or hidden away in cloth bags, the cans and church key openers covered
by sandwiches. Those fans who were lacking would wait until they
passed the two liquor stores on Stanyan Street on the way to the
game. It had become a tradition—the team walking to the game,
followed by the band, the students, and the fans. This year, because
of the publicity that had filled the papers due to my relentless
information releases to all the sports writers, and because of the
obvious brilliance of several of the returning players, there were
over twice as many revelers as there had been the previous year.

Kezar Stadium was built in 1925 with a gift of $100,000 from the estate of Mary Kezar to honor her mother and uncles, who were early San Francisco residents. The city kicked in an additional $200,000, and San Francisco had a state-of-the-art 50,000-seat athletic facility. The opening ceremony in 1925 featured a two-mile race between Paavo Nurmi, the world champion from Finland, and Ville Ritola. The contest was enjoyed by a full house sitting on the hard bench seats.

In 1940, USF started its relationship with Kezar, playing a football game against Stanford in a double-header in which Santa Clara also played Utah. The stadium was built in the southeast corner of Golden Gate Park. Its location put it virtually in the center of the city, which was a plus for any venue. For USF, it was almost like it was a part of the campus. The team would have to walk a single city block to the northeast corner of the park, then through trees and giant ferns on dirt walking paths, past the horseshoe pits, the large dell of fuchsias, and the McLaren Lodge, named after the Scotsman who had developed the park. They would cross Central Drive, which would later be named for John F. Kennedy, and walk along footpaths paralleling Kezar Drive and into the stadium.

There were also disadvantages to Kezar's location, however. There was virtually no parking, not that that was a consideration in 1925, as almost all San Francisco residents used either the buses or the Judah street car that passed two blocks from the entrance. By 1951, a great number of USF alumni had moved from the traditional neighborhoods to the Peninsula or across the Golden Gate Bridge to Marin County. By then, with automobile manufacturers turning wartime production seamlessly to civilian needs, most of the city's residents had cars, and parking was becoming a problem. The other disadvantages had to do with the construction of the stadium itself. The state-of-the-art stadium design of 1925 did not account for many food stands, necessary restrooms, or even comfortable seats. To answer these deficiencies, for professional 49er games, the entrances to the streets with their bars and liquor stores were opened at half-time, allowing the fans to leave and return. This was a boon to the numerous establishments that occupied Stanyan Street as well as the mom-and-pop grocery stores, which seemed to be fifty percent refrigerators filled with six-packs of Lucky Lager, Pabst Blue Ribbon, and Schlitz beer. The unlimited cheap alcohol was more a problem for the 49ers, who had started playing their games on Sundays in 1946. Almost every second half of the professional games ended up marred by fights which cascaded down and over the last disadvantage, the hard wooden benches.

Actually, the benches were not the last problem. That distinction came from the hundreds of seagulls that arrived on cue at the beginning of the third quarter, circling the stands and doing what seagulls do. A popular refrain among grammar school kids in the city who experienced the same phenomenon at their lunchtime was, "I saw a seagull up in the sky—plop. Aren't you glad that cows can't fly?" The seagulls were a problem for USF as well, but the walk to the stadium, drinking on campus, and not opening the gates at half-time took care of the rest.

I believe that the school and church gave this team a sense of purpose bigger than themselves. Kuharich and his staff did their part in boosting the team's confidence and feeling of self-worth, but the Jesuits added a resolve that was bigger than a team, a game, or a season. On the morning of the Dons' opening game, we received a Jesuit blessing. It all felt right, even for those of us who weren't Catholic.

I left the campus early, walking down the hill to the Kezar press room on the stadium's south rim. The stands were already filling, with the large section just to the right and below the press box empty, awaiting the arrival of the students and faculty. The only person occupying the press area was Curley Grieve. I asked him where the others were who would cover the game. He laughed and told me he was it. All my work to hype this team and we got only one reporter, although Grieve was the one with the largest readership.

Curley acted hurt and asked if the *Examiner* wasn't enough, adding that he knew I was worried about this game. I told him again that he would be astounded by what he would see in the next three hours. I mentioned Matson's speed, Scudero's quickness, Marchetti, and Toler, but mostly I told him what I had seen in practice. Brown had been given the okay to pass. Kuharich had added at least ten more pass plays to the playbook. Grieve smiled, took out a cigar, and shoved it in his mouth. "We'll see. We'll talk after the game." I had given him my best shot and I was angry that I had been forced to give it to a single reporter. I steamed out of the press box and went looking for a hot dog.

Two hours before the start of the game, the team came out of the locker room, fully clothed in uniforms, pads, and spikes. They moved up to the grass square on the side of St. Ignatius Church and were greeted by an assembly of students and fans. The band struck up the USF fight song and fell in behind the team and coaches as they moved off toward Kezar. They played continually, except when they crossed Central Drive, where San Francisco's finest motorcycle cops stopped traffic for the procession. The team entered the locker room, which was contained in a small building to the north of the stadium. They would enter the field through a thirty-five-yard tunnel onto the east end zone. The band would go through the Stanyan Street gate with the students, while the rest of the fans sought out the gates nearest their seats, many of which surrounded the student section. Hats on the men was the norm.

San Jose State was USF's first opponent of the year, and they met a Dons squad that was not only hyped up but eager to hit someone other than their own teammates and hit them hard. Curley Grieve wrote the morning of the game, "The University of San Francisco launches its 'year of decision' in football tonight when it faces San Jose State College under Kezar's crown of lights… With honors and trumps in abundance, they didn't get an opportunity to play their hand in a fast league… But the Dons—players, alumni, faculty, and followers—have rebounded with greater determination, fashioned a post-season bowl game objective, and announced an ambition to [using a line I had sent him] 'get under the skin and into the heart' of the city." Grieve would turn out to be prophetic.

All one needed to know about the game could be summed up by noting that the USF defense did not allow a San Jose State first down until there were twelve minutes left in the fourth quarter. The final score was 39 to 2. Matson ran for 127 yards, while Merrill Peacock scored three touchdowns. Bob St. Clair added another six with a pass reception and a short run to the goal line. Brown ended up with 261 passing yards, completing 19 out of 34 passes. The locker room was jubilant as the coaching staff entered after a brief meeting on the field.

With less than five minutes left in the game, I smiled at Curley Grieve. Three other reporters had arrived along with several photographers just before kickoff. Toward the end they were cheering along with the crowd. With five minutes left in the game, I left the press box and took the steps down to where a man in a jacket, a tie, and an outrageous fedora stood in front of the band. We had a quick conversation, the man, who was the band leader, nodding in agreement. I hustled back up to the press box. As the game entered the last two minutes, the band struck up "Goodnight Irene," the Weavers tune that Tringali had played at Corning. The crowd took up the song, standing, arms linked and swaying while singing the lyrics, and a tradition that would grow with each game was born.

Here it is almost thirty-four years later, and I still can't think of that season without hearing that damn song in my head. The first game of the '51 season and it just snowballed from there. It became our unofficial theme song. Everybody loved it except the team we were beating that day.

I went back to the press box where Grieve and the other guys were finishing up their copy for the Saturday paper, promising them more background on the stars the next day, then left to join the team in the locker room. It was crowded, not because of the players but because the room was so small and primitive. The coaches were upstairs in a small office discussing the game before coming down to the team. As I got there, I could hear St. Clair's deep voice, laughing.

"Did I have two or three guys hanging on me for that touchdown? I couldn't tell."

"That's 'cause they all caught your slow butt," said Scudero. "And since they were hanging on back there, there was no way you could see how many."

"Did someone say that was a beautiful pass?" Ed Brown chimed in.

"Defense is the story of the day, boys," said Marchetti, moving to the center of the room while taking off his shirt, his torso a palette of bruises. "Which means I'm sleeping in tomorrow!"

I was hoping to get a few choice quotes that I could fill the papers with prior to the next game against Idaho in Boise when Kuharich walked into the locker room, flanked by both Coach Ryan and Kerr. His eyes narrowed at the laughter; the serious expression on both the coaches' faces showed that they were displeased. As Kuharich started to speak, his normally high-pitched voice rose an octave.

"I'm disgusted. I would have thought that Corning and this year's camp taught you how a team behaves. What I saw out there was no team effort, just a lot of selfishness. If it persists, this team will not achieve success, no matter how many lopsided wins we have this season. I saw almost every one of you play harder when it was your play called than when you were supposed to be blocking—clearing the way for a teammate. Think this over. There will be a practice on Sunday and you better show up with a new attitude." Kuharich turned his back and stomped out of the locker room and back upstairs, leaving the team with their mouths open.

That evening, Marchetti was sitting in his room, nursing his body with ice from the refrigerator in the trainer's room two barracks away. He was reading a paperback book when Toler walked in. A party had been organized to celebrate the victory, and most of the team had gone, but Marchetti had declined the invitation. He had assumed Toler was attending it. He told me about their conversation later.

Toler started to undress, then went over to Marchetti and lifted the spine of the book so that he could read the title: *Heart of Darkness*. Toler was not surprised at Marchetti's choice of literature. He had not gone to the party either but had spent three hours in the library instead.

"You go to the party, Burl?"

"Nah. I'm a library guy. You?"

"I'm already in Father Giambastiani's shithouse. Now, given what Coach said, I thought I better behave."

Toler pulled up a chair and sat down in his underwear. "You know you're driving Father Giambastiani crazy. Are you really here just for football?"

"Nah. It's just that academics is tough for me, but it's what I need most. Football is easy. I never thought about the schooling side so much, let alone professional ball, until Coach Lynn came to the bar. Now with everybody talking about the pros, I'm thinking I'd like to give it a shot. I've got to learn at school and get better at football. I get the coaching stuff easy. The books, not so good."

"You got to keep your studies up. If you have trouble, I can help. We need each other out there. What's that?" asked Toler, pointing to a handle protruding from the pillow on Marchetti's bunk.

"It's a knife." Marchetti pulled an eight-inch blade, still in its canvas sheath, out from beneath the pillow. "It's become a habit. The war left scars on me. I learned early that the bullet that kills you doesn't 'zing,' it 'cracks' … Like blindsiding a quarterback. One day we were moving into this French village. I was just kinda looking around and my buddy tells me to pull my head down. I tell him that the bullets ain't close 'cause those ones crack. He calls me a big goomba and says that I got it wrong, the cracking and the zinging. My buddy didn't make it out that day. I found him laid out in a barn on some straw with his skull half blown away. I could have given a shit about school up till then. I was just scared and hoping to get out alive. All my buddy wanted to do was serve his country and then go to college and get his degree. He's still there and I'm here. It's his knife."

As they were getting ready to turn off the lights and go to sleep, the door burst open and Vince Tringali entered.

"Now that was a party! Scudero was telling a chick that he was gonna be an actor. I told him they already cast the munchkins in *The Wizard of Oz*. Can you believe that clown?"

Marchetti rolled over and pretended to go to sleep. Toler did the same, and Tringali, hearing Scudero, obviously drunk, enter the barracks, turned and helped his teammate to his room. Toler thought it was a good thing that tomorrow was Saturday and they didn't have practice until Sunday.

CHAPTER FIFTEEN

Sunday's practice was brutal. Kuharich paid little attention to the player whose number was called on any play, but his voice rose an octave and a half, with a like increase in decibels, as the session went on. His ire was particularly focused on the players who didn't finish their blocking assignments or didn't follow the play once it had passed them. For over two thirds of the plays, the first string played offense, leaving only half an hour at the end to go over a few defensive alignments. The ball carrier and designated pass catcher were almost ignored unless they made a mistake. At the end of two hours, everyone was exhausted, including the coaches, who were taken up with Coach Kuharich's determination to drill the squad on teamwork rather than individual effort.

I had been given this noisy old rattle-trap of a typewriter. I think it was war surplus. It was better than mine in one important way: it could make four carbon copies and the fourth would be clear enough to read. My personal machine would smear the second.

I don't think I've ever been so excited before or since, getting the word out about our team's potential after that first game. I was even starting to believe the glowing exaggerations I was kicking out like sparks in preparation for our next game against the University of Idaho in Boise. Going on the road was always difficult. That was particularly true in Idaho, where the fans were rabid, and usually large, loud people. I was typing away, lost in a world of inflated stats and outrageous adjectives, when Father Feeley came in and started reading the copy over my shoulder. He liked it, particularly the phrase "The Kezar Wrecking Crew." I was doing the physical finger work, but in reality, the team was writing its own copy.

He asked if I was accompanying the team to Boise, which I was. Coach Kuharich had informed me the day before of that fact. I guess he was happier with me than with the team after that first game. He liked the way I got along with the coaches and had gained the trust of the team. Coach Kuharich had asked that I not write too much about individual stats, except for Matson's, but rather concentrate on team accomplishments whenever possible.

Father Feeley clapped me on the back and told me he was proud of the job I was doing. I replied that the players made it easy, that they were interesting people outside of football. I mean, Burl Toler was well read in the classics. The previous day during practice, the defense was about to go onto the field and he had said to the linebackers, "Cry 'Havoc!' and let slip the dogs of war!" Marchetti, who had seen real war, just looked at him for several seconds and then yelled, "Yeah!" Ollie Matson was a professional-level dancer who had won several competitions around the city. Big Bob St. Clair let everyone who would listen know that his goal in life was to become a politician. Feeley had heard about little Joe Scudero's acting ambitions, as that story had spread from the team to the classroom to the Jesuits in little more than a day. As usual, Scudero was ready to fight anyone who laughed.

Coach Kuharich remained distant and dissatisfied with the team practices for the entire week. He reserved his talks for the coaches, his screams for the players. The team was nearing their limit. I could tell that they were ready to hammer someone if they didn't get to the game soon.

Boise had about 85,000 residents in 1951, and I think that 84,000 of them were rabid football fans. The stands were filled, the day hot. It didn't take long for Kuharich to show that he was still angry about the repeated failure to finish pass plays that he had observed in the first game. After the seventh bench-called running play, Ed Brown had figured it out. He told the players in the huddle they had better block hard and long on running plays, because he had a feeling that was all they were going to see called that day. Matson was the beneficiary; St. Clair and Scudero, who had been the main recipients of Kuharich's wrath during the week of practice, got nothing. Peacock, who'd had a great game against San Jose State, was being punished as guilty by association.

Matson had three touchdowns on 235 yards. He carried the ball 33 times, which left little for the other running backs. Joe Scudero did not get much on offense but showed his worth by scoring the fourth touchdown of the day by virtue of a fifty-eight-yard punt reception.

Perhaps Kuharich's displeasure with the team for not blocking downfield during the week of practice had enabled Matson to have his great day, but on Scudero's runback it showed the price that is often paid for "rock 'em sock 'em" football. Ed Brown as quarterback threw a vicious block that enabled Scudero to break free after catching the punt. Brown was a big man, 6' 2" and 210 pounds—huge for a quarterback in that era—but on that play he wrenched his back, forcing him to the sidelines and placing Bill Henneberry in the lineup to finish the game. It had no effect on the game or score, as Henneberry was more than capable, but it would in the next game against the Camp Pendleton Marines.

The final score was USF 28, Idaho 7. It was the team's second convincing win.

CHAPTER SIXTEEN

A lot had been made of the Dons' weak schedule in 1951, as typi-
fied by Dink Templeton calling it a "freeze-out" by the Pacific
Coast Conference. Often the fact that they were playing a couple
of U. S. military teams—the Marines of Camp Pendleton and
the San Diego Naval Training Center—was cited as evidence
that USF was facing unworthy opponents. What was often forgotten in later years was the fact that it was the beginning of the
Korean War and the draft was in full effect. Many athletes who,
like Marchetti, were on the cusp end of World War II had played
football and entered the pros. In 1951 they became eligible for the
draft. Large training centers in all services had football teams,
and depending on the base commander's competitive nature and
dedication to winning sports teams, they ensured these professional and college players were assigned to their bases. Once at a
station, they were put into Special Services and played for brag-
ging rights and pride against other service teams. There were
many college teams that would not measure up to their talent or
their depth.

As Kuharich looked over the film on the Camp Pendleton
Marines, he saw that it more closely resembled a professional
roster than a college one. Playing for the Marines was Cloyce
Box, who had been named all-pro with the Detroit Lions just
the year before. There was also Joe Cribari, who came close to
becoming an All-American at center at Denver University. Other

ex-pro players were Walt Szot and Bob Burl, at tackle, teamed with Gene Valentine, who played guard for Rice. In the backfield was Charlie Harris from the University of Georgia, a program known for its running backs.

The films supplied by the Marines were of poor quality, showing only one camera angle and often following the ball rather than taking in the whole field. It was more of a highlight film against a poor opponent than the type of game film Kuharich was used to receiving. The coach suspected the quality of the game film was a deliberate strategy by the Marines' head coach. The six players gave them a good core, but Kuharich could see that they lacked depth as well as size and technique in those who filled in the other five spots, both on offense and defense. Of more concern was the injury to Ed Brown. He was not cleared to play, and Kuharich was worried that his injury might hold him out as long as a month. For the present, it meant that Bill Henneberry would have to take over the reins at quarterback with a whole half-quarter of varsity experience. Henneberry was 50 pounds lighter and four inches shorter than Brown and not nearly as accurate a passer, without the arm to be able to pass as far downfield. He did have two qualities that Kuharich had seen and appreciated during the previous two years. The senior backup quarterback was well liked and respected by the team, and he was smart. He was not only book smart, he was football smart. Kuharich knew that if he installed a game plan, Henneberry would follow it. He would be a perfect short-term replacement for Brown. He just hoped that it wouldn't have to be for long.

USF was a small school; it was part of the reason their teams didn't get the respect they deserved. Football and basketball were the two sports that got any recognition because of their ability to put butts in seats. The USF soccer team was to win six national championships under Coach Negoesco, but it was football and basketball that got all the press.

The coaching staff was small as well, the athletic department a close-knit group. I mentioned that I had worked for the basketball team as a graduate assistant; Coach Phil Woolpert had recommended me for the publicity director's position with the football program. Woolpert had just hired a graduating basketball player, Ross Giudice, as an assistant. Ross and I had had a couple of courses together. He was smart, an Accounting major, and I liked him.

Ross showed up in my office two days before we were to play Camp Pendleton at Kezar. Ross was all business and had great time management skills. He would have to have those attributes, as he was teaching at Archbishop Riordan High School, which was across the city, coaching the freshman squad and assisting with the varsity squad. Ross was also managing a family furniture store. His visit seemed casual, but I knew he did everything with a purpose. Finally, he asked about recruiting. I told him that Coach Lynn did most of it, and he would be the one to ask, but Ross said he wanted me to give him some ideas. He didn't want to know how the coaches found the kids or identified them as good players. He wanted to know how, once the coaches had identified prospects they really wanted, they convinced them to come to USF.

Coach Woolpert had given Ross the job of scouting the East Bay for talent and serving as the first recruiting contact for any individuals who showed college-level ability. He had seen a young player in a couple of games playing for McClymonds High School in Oakland, and Ross believed that the young man, although raw and untutored, had the potential to become an excellent college player with the right coaching. He didn't want to blow it with this kid, whose name was Russell—William Felton Russell.

I related the story about Gino being recruited in the bar in Pittsburgh, telling it from both Coach Lynn's side and Gino's. We laughed about how two people seeing the same thing could have such different feelings about the event, when both coach and recruit badly wanted the same outcome. I also gave him the story about Hal Sachs's recruitment in Manhattan Beach. Coach Lynn had gone down to Los Angeles and rented a car. He was told that Sachs would be at the beach surfing in the afternoon, and he wasn't really thinking when he wore a suit and tie down from San Francisco. He had planned to talk to him at the beach and afterward visit with his parents at their home, then take the last flight home out of Orange County Airport.

As Lynn told me, "I got to the beach and immediately felt the stares. There were about twenty surfers on boards in the water and a similar number on the beach or skid-boarding on the expended shore break. Most were young and skinny. I walked toward the water, feeling the soft sand ooze over the tops of my shoes. I asked the first person I came to if he knew Hal Sachs. The guy was small, like most of the rest of those I could see on the beach. I was beginning to doubt the scouting reports we had received from down south.

"The kid waved a hand indiscriminately toward the water, which helped me not at all. 'He's the one doing tandem,' he added, turning back to waxing his board. I still couldn't pick out Sachs. Then far out I saw someone catch a wave, and as soon as he was on it, hoist a girl in a two-piece suit who had been standing directly in front of him first onto his shoulders and then above his head. He rode the wave almost to the shore, then slung the girl around his back and into the waist-deep water. As the girl came ashore, the kid I had talked to walked down and pointed in my direction. She turned and said something to Sachs, then started up the beach toward me. She had looked petite at the water's edge standing next to Sachs, but as she came toward me I realized she was a big girl, a very big girl. 'You looking for Hal? He'll be up in a minute,' she said in a deep, husky voice as she reached me.

"I had the mental vision of Sachs throwing her around. Standing next to me, I saw that she must have been nearly six feet tall. I had no difficulty offering the chiseled, bronze Hal Sachs a scholarship when he finally finished taking care of the oversized board he was riding and joined the girl with a large, handsome smile." Lynn returned home with a signed National Letter of Intent and an even bigger smile. He was not in the least bit worried that he still had not seen the kid play football.

Ross told me that that this story was exactly the kind of thing he'd hoped to hear. He commented on the fact that there was humor in the stories of each of the first contacts. It was going to be a little different with Russell. It was not possible for a college coach to be in the stands for any high school game without the coaches, all the assistants, and the entire team knowing about it by tip-off. If the coaches didn't recognize the college scout, some spectator would, and it would get back to the bench, usually by a whispered word on the way to the bathroom or to get a drink and popcorn. The coach would usually inform his players. It was a double-edged sword. The coach hoped that the players would up their play and win without trying to take over the game or ignoring teamwork for individual stats. Russell was aware that Ross had watched him previously, and by now he knew him by sight. Ross wanted their face-to-face interview to be a positive experience. In Ross's favor, the kid seemed unknown to other college scouts. He had seen no other coaches around, and the McClymonds coach had told him, if he could be believed, that there had been no interest in the 6'9" newcomer up till now. As it turned out, the stance that the football team would take later that year had a solidifying effect on Russell's attending USF.

I had one more story that could help Ross, one that I had just learned from Coach Lynn after Ollie Matson's 233-yard game against Idaho. I had asked the coach if the recruiting of Matson had been difficult. I knew that he had made a name for himself at San Francisco City College and been sought after by several coaches, but I had no idea who had made first contact or if

Matson had been secured before his teammate, Toler. If Giudice wasn't going to recruit Russell in a bar or on a beach, then I thought that the recruiting of Matson would be interesting for him to hear about, since it had taken a more conventional path.

It was no secret that the San Francisco City College program was like Candy Land for college recruiters. Year after year the team was in the running for the mythical national junior college championship. Year after year dozens of players were offered Division I scholarships after playing for City. Matson had been courted since his first year, Toler somewhat later, after coaches watching Matson kept noticing that City's opponents never got any yardage over the left side where Toler played and after a while just stopped trying. Kuharich had even scouted a few of Matson's games personally and had invited him to visit USF, which he had done with his mother, Gertrude Matson. The visit went well, and Kuharich was hopeful. He was helped in his recruiting of Matson, who should have been the number one priority on any college's list, by the fact that Ollie was Black. At that time in the PAC, teams had few Black players on their rosters. Although Pacific had a Black all-conference running back, in the South there were none, and it was highly unusual on the east coast as well in 1951. This was just fine with Kuharich. It gave him a better chance of recruiting the player. Time was drawing near, though, and they still had not signed Matson. Kuharich sent Coach Lynn over to the Matson house to try to secure Matson's commitment.

Gertrude Matson happened to be looking out the window as Brad Lynn strode up the steps of their small flat. She opened the door before he reached the doorbell and welcomed him in. It was the first time the coach had been in the modest, clean house. The coach could hear heavy breathing interspersed with soft grunts coming from the hallway leading to the back of the house. Mrs. Matson sat Coach Lynn in the front room, asking him if he would like a cup of coffee. After he thanked her, she

excused herself, busying herself in the kitchen before returning with Ollie, who had obviously had been working out. He
was dressed in a sweat-stained T-shirt and a pair of shorts. His
feet were in a pair of low-cut black Converse with no socks
showing.

"Sorry, Coach Lynn. Mom said you had called and that you
might drop by, but she didn't tell me the time."

"When we talked, we didn't set a time. Is this all right? I'm
not interrupting anything, am I?"

"Not at all, Coach. I was just working out. What can I do for
you?"

"Coach Kuharich sent me over to ask if there's anything else
you want to know about our offer. It's getting to the point where
you have to give us a firm commitment or we must start looking
seriously at other options."

"I'm almost ready to commit, Coach. I think I just need a
little more time."

Gertrude was soft-spoken and talked to her son adult to
adult. "Ollie, I'm glad you stopped visitin' all those big schools.
I think you should decide on that little college on the hill. I can
walk a few blocks and keep an eye on you."

"It's a university, Mom. I really like USF. No other place made
me feel so wanted. I just would like a little more time."

"Time? Time to do what, be some boxer, like that man Joe
Louis? I like Coach Kuharich. He's a serious man. He's serious
about you getting a good education. He's serious about his players. There's truth in his eyes."

Matson looked hard at his mother, frowning. "It has to be my
decision, Mom." Ollie was plainly unhappy that this conversation was occurring in front of Coach Lynn. "Is it just because the
school is nearby and I'll be here to help you?"

"Now boy, you think we've worked this hard to get you and
your sister out of Texas for nuthin'? A good religious school is

where you need to be. I don't need to worry about kids screaming stuff at you. And I like those monks."

"They're priests, Mom. Catholic priests."

Brad Lynn was becoming embarrassed at being a spectator to this private conversation. It was not what he had expected. "Ollie," he said, trying to alter the direction of the conversation. "All recruits have trouble pulling the string. That is particularly true of the really good players. I've never met one who wasn't somewhat unsure at this point in the process. After all, it is a decision that will mean the next two years of your life and will affect your life after college, too. Your decision should be equally good for you and the school. But I can tell you this. There is no university that wants you more or has watched you play more games than USF. There isn't another school that will treat you better or where you will get a better education. Your mom is right."

Brad Lynn got up and thanked Mrs. Matson for the coffee, holding out his hand to Ollie. They shook, and Ollie turned to look at his mother.

"Coach, I give you my commitment. I'll play for you at USF. Can I ask if my teammate, Burl Toler, is being seriously recruited?"

"Yes, he is. I believe that Coach has an appointment with Burl on campus in two days and will offer him a scholarship then. I would ask that you don't tell Burl that last part until it happens, though. I am happy you made your decision. I believe with all my heart that USF and the team we are building will be the perfect fit for you. Still, I suggest that you take your time and come in tomorrow. I'll have the papers ready for you and you can bring them home and sign them."

As I related the story of Matson's recruitment to Ross Giudice, he smiled and saw the relevance. Recruit with humor and honesty, but without fail, also recruit the parents. Ross asked why Lynn didn't have the National Letter of Intent and scholarship offer with him when he went to see the Matsons. He had picked up on Lynn's oversight. The National Letter of Intent committed the player to the university, while the scholarship committed the school and the monetary award to the recruit. Both were binding. Lynn should have been carrying the documents. He also realized his own mistake. He had no knowledge of Russell's family. In all the talks with the coach, he had not heard of his parents being near.

Ross thanked me and departed, leaving me to pound out another paragraph of hyperbole about our team and the upcoming game against the red-and-yellow-clad Camp Pendleton Marines. A year later, Ross signed Russell and another player from San Francisco named K. C. Jones. Not bad for a first year's recruiting effort. Between the two recruits, they would have 21 NBA Championship rings in later years. K. C. would achieve one more than Russell, which is always good knowledge for winning a drink at a bar.

As it turned out, despite trying, I could not have oversold our squad to the press. The final score that afternoon was 26 to 0 in favor of the Dons in front of almost 7,000 fans on a sunny Sunday at Kezar. Ollie ran for two touchdowns in the first quarter, one of 14 yards and another of 66 yards that was set up when Joe Scudero almost decapitated the Marine defensive back to spring Matson free for his jaunt. Roy Giorgi picked up yet another interception in the second half, running it in for our third score. Despite the score, it was a hard-fought game, particularly on the line. Kuharich kept Henneberry primarily on the ground. The defense was magnificent, as performed by Marchetti, Toler, and the suddenly defensive-minded St. Clair. The Marines gained 64 yards on the ground, but they were stopped behind the line for 111 yards, giving them a total yardage of minus 47 yards. Matson was a big part of that, as defensively he was assigned to cover Cloyce Box, the former all-pro receiver for the Detroit Lions. Box couldn't get free of Matson, and their quarterback, Hamer, soon stopped throwing to him. In the last quarter, Henneberry was given a little more leeway and he lofted a pass of forty yards that McLaughton caught and ran with untouched for 26 yards for the final touchdown.

My roommate the previous year, Pierre Salinger, had started writing a piece or two for the *Chronicle*. He interviewed Coach Kuharich after the game and it was printed the next day along with the account of the game. Kuharich called Matson the best football player in the nation, and his opinion was echoed by Major Ralph Cormany, the Marines' head coach. Funny, Pierre was always trying to get me to go into politics. He insisted there was much more to write about in politics than in football, but he started his career by writing about sports for the *Chronicle*. What Pierre didn't report was that the smile Kuharich wore at game's end was not because of the final score but because his tirade after the first game had, at the end of the third quarter, finally taken hold. The Dons were playing as a team, not as individuals. They were blocking for each other, helping on defense, and taking pure joy in their accomplishment in shutting out the Marines.

CHAPTER SEVENTEEN

September and October, along with June, are the best weather months in San Francisco. The average temperature is about 69 degrees. In San Jose, which is 70 miles south at the bottom of the Bay, it averages over 10 degrees warmer. The nights are also warmer, as San Jose is protected from the Pacific Ocean by the coastal range of mountains that span from Daly City, just south of San Francisco, all the way to Santa Cruz.

The San Jose coaching staff and players had smarted after the first game played at Kezar. They now felt they had the gist of the Dons' style of play and their personnel. After being blitzed by Ed Brown's aerial show the first go-round, the coaches stacked the defensive backfield, dropping the linebackers into coverage as well. Therefore, after a few unsuccessful pass attempts, Brown, now returning at quarterback, started calling running plays. The result was again two first-quarter touchdowns. Matson on that day had three by himself, Toler a defensive safety for 2 points. Joe Scudero added another on a five-yard dash around end and helped with the rest as the holder for Hal Sachs's extra-point kicks. After the game, Brown admitted to Scrap Iron that his back was still stiff and sore. He had passed only ten times with as many interceptions as completions, two for only five yards, as the Dons' offense ran one play after another and defeated the Spartans 42–7 on Columbus Day.

We had eight days between the team's fourth game at San Jose State and the fifth game with Fordham in New York. So far we had racked up impressive victories, but it was unlikely that many had noticed on the east coast, or, as Coach Kuharich pointed out, in the smoke-filled board rooms that controlled the major bowl games, which were all in the south. The Fordham game was pivotal, as the team wanted to avenge the defeat USF had suffered the year before, but more importantly because of the power of the New York press. USF might not have a game in the south (not counting the three they would have in southern California), but people in the south certainly read the New York papers. Over the first month of the season, it had become apparent from reading the city newspapers that an invitation to a post-season bowl game was the only thing that would likely save the USF football program. Nothing had been said by the university about the possibility of suspending the football program, but it had been mentioned several times by different reporters. It was not clear where they were getting their information, or if it was just common sense that led them to their conclusions, but whatever the source, it was a given that a bowl game was more than important to the program's future.

I went to see Father Feeley on Sunday afternoon. I chose that as a start because I felt that what I wanted to propose was more a university concern than a football concern. It helped that Father Feeley was a strong supporter of athletics, especially football. I started by telling him that the week before the Fordham game would be a waste if I spent it on the west coast. I told him that I had sold our players and the team before the season to all the skeptical local sports reporters, and now they had taken up the beat of the drum. They had seen the team on fire through four wipeouts and I didn't need to fan the flame anymore. They had full bios on all the team members and enough quotes from the coaching staff to last them the entire season. What I needed to do now was convince the New York beat writers.

Feeley knew that the eastern college teams were covered fully. Whether it was because of the three-hour time difference or the arrogance of the writers' belief that good football and good football writing stopped at the Appalachians, west coast teams were not covered. I told him that I was the publicity director, not a coach, and I would be of more service if I was in New York the week prior to the game. To my delight, he agreed and said he would talk to Kuharich. If Kuharich agreed, he would free up the money to send me off six days prior to the team's departure. I knew on a visceral level that this was the right way to spend my time and energy. What I didn't fully grasp at the time was that the trip would change the direction of my life.

Kuharich gave me the go-ahead, telling Father Feeley that it would give him more time with the team, as I was always interviewing them for one reason or another. As soon as I got the word, I arranged for a flight later that afternoon and had Pierre Salinger drive me down to the San Francisco airport. I had no time to go to the business office to get a cash advance, so I had to use my own money to get the ticket. I asked Pierre to talk to Father Feeley and ask him to send a money order to my hotel on Monday.

The flight took almost seven hours, most of which I spent sleeping but none too well. I was so excited about going to New York that I kept waking up and having trouble getting back to sleep. It didn't help that I was in a middle seat in coach, the only thing available with such short notice, not that Father Feeley would have paid for anything better, and the older lady in the window seat had to use the restroom every hour and a half. The breakfast they served aided in settling my stomach and counteracting the three cups of coffee served by a very pleasant stewardess. By the time I retrieved my luggage and hailed a cab, it was seven-thirty. I had packed my only suit and my sport coat with a single pair of slacks, figuring I could mix and match and get by with three shirts and seven sets of socks and underwear. I checked into the hotel the team would be staying at later in the week, took a long shower, and wrote down the things I hoped to accomplish in the next seven days. It was an easy task, as I had planned and gone over it several times in my mind while trying to get back to sleep on the plane.

I had learned that newspaper men tended to be creatures of the night. They were always on deadlines for the morning editions. The editors and staff were usually in place in the morning, but those were not the people I needed to contact. I took the players' bios out of my briefcase along with a one-page synopsis of the first four games and stacked them on the desk. Then I lay down on the bed and tried to snatch a few hours' sleep. My plan was simple—go after Grantland Rice.

Grantland Rice was renowned as the dean of America's sports writers. In 1951 he was celebrating his 50th year in the business. Originally from Tennessee, he had come to New York in 1914 with a degree from Vanderbilt and a propensity for writing prose that made the games and individuals into epic battles and heroes. His description of the 1924 football game between Notre Dame and Army had cemented his position, and it is still probably the most famous piece of prose ever written about sports. In it he dubbed the Notre Dame backfield the "Four Horsemen of the Apocalypse." I had memorized the paragraph in an assignment for a speech class at USF: "Outlined against a blue-gray October sky, the Four Horsemen rode again. In dramatic lore they are known as Famine, Pestilence, Destruction and Death. These are only aliases. Their real names are Stuhldreher, Miller, Crowley and Layden. They formed the crest of the South Bend cyclone before which another fighting Army football team was swept over the precipice at the Polo Grounds yesterday afternoon as 55,000 spectators peered down on the bewildering panorama spread on the green plain below."

I can still recite it to this day. It was my hope that I could get Grantland to come to the game and write similar prose about Matson, Toler, Marchetti, and Brown. If I could get him to attend and fill him with information about "all the way Ollie," the other scribes would follow. I slept for almost four hours.

The hotel that had been arranged was only about ten blocks from Times Square. When I saw New York City for the first time, I realized that everything I had done in my life had led me to this moment. I knew for a fact that it was where I was meant to be.

I went to the *Tribune* building and headed upstairs to make my introductions to the sports staff. It was three times the size of the *Chronicle*, San Francisco's largest newspaper. I didn't expect to find Rice there, and I was correct. Most of the columnists looked at me like I was from outer space. Some didn't even shake my hand when I offered it. The younger reporters were friendlier, but only slightly so. I left a set of the bios and a list of Ollie's accomplishments so far that season in Rice's call box. I also asked for a phone number where I might contact Rice. The floor editor almost laughed. I asked what time he normally came in and was told that he almost never did that anymore, sending in most of his columns by phone. I just kept a smile on my face and told them I would try again the next day.

As I left the floor and went to the elevator, a young copy boy stepped in with me. As soon as the door closed, he turned to me, gave his name as Jesse Salcedo, and said that his parents lived in Mill Valley, just across the Golden Gate Bridge from San Francisco. They had kept him up on the Dons games and he was looking forward to the game with Fordham. Then he lowered his voice and told me that Mr. Rice had dinner every Tuesday night at Max's with some other reporters. I thanked him for the information and promised him a ticket to the game. As soon as the door opened, he left in a hurry, giving the impression that we had never talked. The kid would have his ticket at Will Call, and I would be at Max's the next night.

CHAPTER EIGHTEEN

Max's was somewhere between a hangout for upper-class sports figures and a four-star European cuisine restaurant complete with a seriously snobby maître d'. I wished I had asked Jesse what time Grantland Rice usually ate. I went through the dining area three times from the bar to the restroom but did not see any sign of Rice. I was nursing my third three-dollar beer when I saw him come in and watched the maître d' snap to attention, bringing him to a table against the far wall. He was accompanied by a short fat man with combed-back black hair. The two of them reminded me of Abbott and Costello as they were led to the table. I debated whether to bring my beer, finally deciding that despite its lofty price, I should leave it at the bar. Instead, I took a last deep swallow, bolstering my courage, and made my way to Rice's table.

Rice was 71 years old but he sat bolt upright and looked like the athlete he had once been at Vanderbilt. He had a drink in front of him that had been delivered apparently without anyone taking the order. His companion couldn't have been more different. He spread himself over his chair, leaning on the table with both elbows, grasping a tumbler of amber liquid filled to the halfway mark.

I tried to keep my voice steady as I introduced myself to Mr. Rice as Pete Rozelle from the University of San Francisco. Mr. Rice offered his hand but remained seated. His companion just grunted and nodded. I asked if he had received the press clippings, bios, and list of Matson's accomplishments that I had left for him on Monday. He replied that he had not been at the paper that day but had been told that a young fellow from San Francisco had left some papers for him. Then, to my surprise, he asked me to take a chair and join them.

He introduced his companion as Harold Rosenthal. I recognized the name as a columnist for the *New York Herald Tribune*. Rosenthal was younger than Rice but still a senior member of the media. Despite the invitation to join them, both remained somewhat aloof and skeptical of me.

I was a little star-struck, and all the fine words I had rehearsed in my head prior to coming to the table had disappeared from my mind. I was sitting there, at a loss for words for once in my life, when Rosenthal saved me.

"Let me guess. You want to recommend one or more of your players to Grantland for his All-American picks, eh?"

That freed me up, and I laughed, saying that would be nice, but what I wanted was for both of them to come to the Fordham game and see Ollie Matson for themselves. Rice, after offering me a seat, had said nothing, studying the wine list instead of paying attention to what Rosenthal and I were discussing. I started rattling off some of Ollie's stats: ten touchdowns in the first four games, leading the nation in running yards. Still Rice did not glance away from the wine list.

Rosenthal gave a soft snicker and asked me if I really thought an All-American could come from such a little school. "I suggest that you watch him play," I responded. "He deserves all that has been written about him—all-the-way Ollie. He's the real deal, Mr. Rosenthal." I pulled out a copy of the information I had left at the *Tribune* and handed it to Rosenthal. Grantland Rice remained like a statue, his eyes half closed, almost asleep. I was getting frustrated at his inattention. "We play Fordham this weekend. I ask that you come and see for yourself."

Without looking up from the wine list, Rice spoke. He had a cultured voice, a soft drawl that mostly concealed his Tennessee upbringing. "There are many games this weekend, young man. Mine is a national column, not a local."

I tried to read his face but it was hidden behind the wine list. I told him that the USF - Fordham game would be the best of them all, and the most significant nationally. He still had not looked in my direction. Finally, I gave up any hint of subtlety and flat out asked him what it would take to get him to watch the game.

For the first time Rice lowered the wine list and looked at me, then shot a subtle glance back at the wine list. I was just getting started in the business but I read the old man's signal loud and clear. I knew it probably meant that I would have to sleep in the lobby for the next two nights, but there was only one thing to do. I signaled the waiter and told him I would like to purchase Mr. Rice's favorite bottle of wine for the table. I was rewarded as Rice put down the wine list and smiled. It was my introduction to sports journalism New York style, and one of the cheapest lessons I ever learned. By the end of the bottle, I had promised to pick Rice and Rosenthal up and drive them across the river to the game.

I spent the next three days touting the Dons to the sports writers' fraternity in New York. After getting Rice's commitment, the rest was much like San Francisco. It cost me a few lunches and several beers, but nothing that would raise eyebrows on an expense account, other than Rice's $32 bottle of Château Margaux. Once the writers found out that the game was worthy of Grantland Rice's attention, they all asked for press credentials, which I was more than happy to arrange. It looked like there would be a full box at the game.

Coach Kuharich brought the team in two full days before the game. He was more worried about the three-hour time difference than the cost of putting up the squad for an extra night. He woke me up at 8:30 in the morning, first with a phone call from the lobby, then minutes later with a knock on the door. I probably would have slept till noon, as the night before had been a late one with many of the beers that were to appear on my expense account purchased that evening. I pulled on my pants and a clean shirt, went into the bathroom, squirted some toothpaste on a brush, and started brushing my teeth as I went to the door to let the coach in. I made the motion that I was in the bathroom as he entered, hoping it looked like I was already up when he called. What I needed was to cover my morning breath, which was bad enough for me to smell. When I came out, the coach was already sitting in one of the two chairs in the room. I grabbed a few of my clothes off the floor and apologized, citing an evening with the New York press as my excuse, threw the clothes in a drawer, and sat down on the bed.

Kuharich wanted a full report on my contacts over the last four days. I knew he had only half bought in when Feeley had recommended me as a full-time staff publicist a little over four months ago. I think he was surprised at the response the local papers had given his squad prior to the season starting. He liked the way that I had arranged interviews for him and prepped him on what they would most likely ask. I believed that he now accepted me and my value to the team. He wanted to know what to expect in the days before the game and who the heavy hitters were. When he was at Notre Dame, there was no need to bait the press. The Irish were always big news; the publicist's job was mostly to restrict access to the players and coaches to a specific timetable, rather than serve them up on a platter like I had done in San Francisco. As I finished recounting the numerous columnists I had interacted with and gave my recommendations as to whom he should grant interviews, he was pleased.

"Great job, Pete," he said. "This game is the most important one we will have this season. Win or lose, we'll have more coverage here than at all the other games combined. This is the big leagues. You've done an excellent job priming the pump—better than I had hoped. There are already two requests for interviews with me at the reception desk and three more for Ollie. I think I'll refuse the ones for Ollie. He would rather let his play answer questions, and I don't want him tired or thinking too much. There is one thing you need to know, though. The coaches and I have been discussing things this last week, and I need you to get up to speed on what we've decided. I'm going to talk with Scooter and I'd like you to be there. In fact, I'd like to call him up here now and get it out of the way before practice. Are you okay with that?"

Moments later I was opening the door for Scudero. Coach motioned him to the remaining chair while I returned to my spot on the bed. I still didn't know what this was about or how it concerned me.

"I didn't do it!" Scudero said upon sitting down.

Kuharich laughed.

"Am I in trouble?" asked a confused Scudero.

"No, Joe! Not at all. We have to make some changes, that's all."

"Coach, it was Tringali's idea ... I've never been to a place like that before ..."

"Scooter, you've done real good out there," said Kuharich, paying no attention to Scudero. "This is about Ollie."

The coach might not have registered it, but I would find out later what Tringali had done that made Scudero so nervous.

Scudero drew back a little on the chair, obviously tense. "Coach, I have no problem with Negroes."

"No one said you did," said Kuharich. "He needs to carry the ball more."

I finally got the gist of what Kuharich was trying to get across and why he wanted me there. Because he was Black and playing in a small program on the west coast, Matson would need overwhelming numbers if he was to be awarded the post-season honors he deserved.

"He needs to carry the ball more if he's going to have a real chance to make All-American. It would be a first for our school."

"They let Jesuit students do that? Be All-Americans?" asked Scudero, still confused.

"Yes, and Ollie has a chance, but he needs more yards. He needs the ball in his hands more. Do you have a problem with that?"

Scudero clenched his fists, looking down at the floor, not answering. I thought he was going to explode. He had performed well in the last two games, both on offense and defense. He was averaging over ten yards a carry. On any other team, he would be the major running threat. I remember Coach looking at me like he was ready for an outburst as well.

Kuharich began to speak again. "Scooter. You're still a key part of my—"

Scudero interrupted him. "Coach, you've given me a chance to play with some amazing guys … an opportunity to learn. I'm a pretty good player, maybe even a great player. In high school I had to do everything myself. Here we kinda, you know … blend. Ollie, though, he's special. I have no problem helping him get what he deserves." Without waiting for an answer, Scudero, the feistiest player on the squad, got up and left the office.

CHAPTER NINETEEN

I parked my rental car behind the team bus and placed my staff pass on the windshield. If I expected to impress Grantland Rice, I was mistaken. As we approached the entry gate, I pulled my three passes from my pocket. As I did, Rice, who was at my shoulder, said, "Hi, Johnny. How is your wife getting along?"

The gate attendant was middle-aged with the shoulders of an offensive tackle and what had to be a 19-inch neck. "She's doing much better, thank you. She'll be thrilled you remembered her, Mr. Rice. Are these two with you?"

Receiving a nod from Rice, the man waved us through without asking for the passes, which I was trying to sneak back into my coat pocket. I followed Rice along the corridor with Harold Rosenthal following, a cigar stuck between his teeth. As we climbed the stairs toward the press box, I could not help but be struck by the view over the south end zone. It was purposely built lower than either of the sideline stands, allowing a panoramic view of Manhattan across the river. As we reached the level of the press box, we stopped, allowing Rosenthal to catch up with us, his weight and the cigar taking their toll during our ascent of three flights of stairs.

As we waited, I heard a loud voice speaking in a heavy Bronx accent. I couldn't pick up the first part of what was said, but it ended with, "Can you believe that kid from San Francisco?" This was followed by laughter from the others already in the box.

If I wasn't intimidated before, I felt about two feet tall at that moment. Grantland Rice didn't seem to hear the comment, or if he did, he gave no response.

As we entered the press box, all the laughter stopped, but I was certain it was more about Grantland Rice entering in front of me looking like a monarch surveying his domain than it was about my presence. A red-faced Harold Rosenthal followed me in. There were two empty chairs in the front row, the favored spots in any press box I had ever seen because the front wall at desk level offered a convenient place for coffee cups and other beverages. Grantland sat down in one and motioned for me to take the other. Rosenthal stood behind the reporter who was sitting on my other side; he appeared to be a few years younger than I was. He looked back, saw Rosenthal looking down on him, and quickly picked up his portable typewriter and moved to the back row. Rosenthal sat down, taking the spot next to the one that had obviously been reserved for him next to Rice. He spread across his area and most of mine. Now situated, both put paper into their typewriters, which had been set up for them by junior members of their respective staffs, and watched the introductions of the teams on the field. Half the seats had typewriters in front of them, the others notebooks.

I was trying to play it cool, but as several reporters came over to shake Rice's hand, asking his opinion on the upcoming game, I felt as nervous as I had at the first game at Kezar, when I had worried that no reporters would show up besides Curly Grieve.

The teams gathered on the field. The Dons had won the coin toss and Ollie Matson and Joe Scudero were lined up on the goal line as deep returners. The Fordham kicker kicked the ball high and deep, slightly to Scudero's side of the field. Matson moved to his left, while Scudero moved up to the ten-yard line to block. Matson caught the ball, starting with a hard cut to his right behind Scudero, and fumbled the ball.

"NO!" I yelled, jumping to my feet and almost toppling Rosenthal's typewriter. I was horror-stricken. All the build-up, all the work and plans, even bringing Grantland Rice personally to the game: it all seemed to go down the drain with that one dropped ball. I was about to yell again when Ollie gracefully bent, gathered in the ball on its first bounce, and immediately reversed directions, cutting to his left as Scudero leveled the first Fordham man down the field. Scooter's technique was unusual. Most downfield blockers waited for contact, stationary so that the runner could decide which way to cut. Scudero instead ran at the player full throttle. Mass plus velocity, he made up for his lack of size with his speed and quickness. It was his secret, and Matson knew what he would do. That man destroyed, Ollie made two defenders miss on his own, cutting down the sideline in front of Kuharich, who dropped his clipboard and was rocked from the side by Coach Jim Ryan. There was one last Fordham defender who had a shot at Ollie with a good angle, but Ollie saw him and added speed that made the would-be tackler look like he was running in mud. He leaped, his body fully extended, his arm grasping, his hands looking for Ollie but finding only air.

I lost it again, yelling, "Yes! Yes! Yes!" Ten seconds later the field was littered with Fordham players, their white jerseys and black-banded stockings on the grass as Ollie stood in the end zone.

I realized that I was still standing, completely blocking the view of the reporters in the two rows behind me, and everyone was looking in my direction, including Grantland Rice. The press box is normally a quiet place during game play, the only sound that of the typewriters chattering away at fifty words a minute. There I was, standing, shouting like a maniacal fan. I slowly sat down, snickers from the front row and full-out laughter from the back making my face turn red with humiliation. I was barely able to say in a low voice to Grantland, "All-the-way Ollie." He sniffed in acknowledgement. The only thing that kept me from slinking out of the press box was that after the laughter subsided, the room sounded like an eighth-grade typing class, the previous quiet completely blown with the clacking of keys striking paper at a furious rate. Next to me the typewriter of Rosenthal joined the raucous sound of the other reporters, recording the opening 94-yard kickoff return.

The game quickly came down to a hard-fought physical struggle, with Fordham's players trying again and again to establish their running game and just as often being thwarted by Marchetti, Toler, Hillig, Thomas, St. Clair, and Sachs. They would eventually run for only 61 total net yards for the entire game. Finally, Fordham scored on a field goal and had to kick off to the Dons again. This time the ball was kicked directly to Scudero who, according to Kuharich's game plan, moved up to block, allowing Ollie to catch the ball on the ten-yard line. Again Ollie fumbled the ball, and again scooped it up without breaking stride. This time I didn't yell, although I had to catch myself. Instead I heard an audible intake of breath from those in the press box. Again Ollie ran around, through, and away from Fordham's defenders to score standing up for his second touchdown of the quarter, this one for 90 yards.

After my humiliating performance on Ollie's first score, I didn't say anything, just sat there and smiled as if 90-yard runbacks after fumbles were an everyday occurrence. I could feel the stares of the others in the press box, perhaps expecting another outburst from the kid from San Francisco. I remember sneaking a look at Grantland, who would type a sentence, read it, think for a bit, and type again. Harold Rosenthal had his cigar out and drooping as he stared at the field, his mouth open.

Unable to generate any ground game, the Fordham Rams went to the air with some success and a punting average of just under 50 yards, giving them good field position to start their drives. It took a fake handoff to Matson and a three-yard run following the 208-pound halfback's block to score Joe Scudero, making it a 32 to 26 USF win.

Rice and Rosenthal got their own rides back to the city after they had phoned in their stories. They did not speak about the game, other than to thank me for the ride over and congratulate me on the win. Another writer, Will Grimsley, came up to me and asked if I could arrange an interview with Coach Kuharich. We went down to the visitor locker room, where several reporters were already waiting to get comments from the staff and the team. Most wanted to speak to Ollie, but as quiet as he was, I knew they would leave disappointed. Coach Kuharich, on the other hand, was as expansive as I had ever seen him after a game. He gave Grimsley a full ten minutes, talking mostly about Matson. He said that if Ollie were playing at a big-time school like Notre Dame or Michigan, he would be recognized as one of the greats, which of course he was. You remember when I was general manager of the Los Angeles Rams, I traded for him, giving up thirteen players. The press had seen him run back two kickoffs for touchdowns totaling 184 yards in the first quarter alone. They did not need much convincing.

We left New York the next day, after collecting morning papers. One article bothered me at first, but then as I read it a second time, I understood that it was a personal message from Harold Rosenthal to me. He wrote at the end of his article, "Rozelle should have his stripes removed for not telling the members of the fourth estate more about this extraordinary runner." At dinner that first night I'd noticed that Rosenthal had pocketed the packet I had put together about Ollie. It was Rosenthal's New York way of telling me I had done a good job and making fun of himself for not believing a word of it. Harold and I later became good friends. When I moved the NFL headquarters here to New

York, I brought him in to work for me. I still have the article framed and hanging on the wall right over there.

Rozelle pointed to the wall to the right of his desk and noticed the time. "Jim, I don't know what gotten into me. It's late and I'm only halfway through the season. Do you have anything going on tomorrow? I think I'd like to continue to tape the rest of this story. It has to be told. I have a feeling it will become more important as time goes on. Say 9:30 tomorrow?"

CHAPTER TWENTY

The next morning at 9:20, Jim Kensil entered the elevator at 410 Park Avenue, and before the doors shut was surprised by the same woman he had seen the previous day entering as the doors had started to close. She hesitated at the floor selection, and seeing that the light was already on for floor 50, turned and gave Kensil a brittle smile. The lift ride for once was a short one, with no one getting on all the way to their destination. As the elevator reached the 50th floor, Jim let the woman exit first, and again they both turned right. He scrutinized her as she walked down the hall in front of him, but this time she turned as she passed the NFL office and saw Kensil watching her. Despite his years, he blushed. He couldn't get to the NFL offices fast enough.

Rozelle was already at his desk, working on the reel-to-reel tape recorder, as Joe was waved in by the receptionist.

"Jim. This is all ready to go. Thanks for coming in. It's much easier to talk with someone than it is to just dictate a story. Have you had breakfast?"

He had, and I was eager to get this recorded. It was not so much the '51 team's season that was the story. What had happened after the final game and in the years since—that was the story. As the season wore on, there were several significant games, or perhaps only parts of games, that were important in demonstrating both the character of the team and the character of the individual players on the team.

I had not forgotten Scudero's nervousness when Coach had told him about his decision to give Ollie some of his carries. It took a while to get the story because the players clammed up when I asked what Scooter had meant in naming Tringali. Vince, having been born and raised in North Beach, was friendly with many of the club owners and managers. This extended to friendship with some of the female performers and sex workers the area was known for. North Beach was a wild place to grow up, and Tringali's personality reflected it. During the ten-day break, Vince had organized a team party on the second story of one of the strip clubs.

The bottom floor held an entrance that opened into the bar, where there was a stage and a small raised platform on which an all-woman band blasted out blues and boogie-woogie songs of surprisingly good quality. Tringali was the first one through the door, waving to the piano player, who without missing a beat started playing a boogie-woogie version of "Goodnight Irene." She began singing verses in a husky voice that was perfect for the setting as the rest of the team filtered in and up the steps to the room above. Twenty minutes later, the band took a break and the piano player, whose name was Wendy, came upstairs with the saxophone player and started entertaining the players. Fifteen members of the team were drinking beer and enjoying themselves, listening to the music, as two performers came on stage and started a slow strip tease to the musical accompaniment. One of the performers beckoned to the players to come on stage and dance with her as she stripped. No one took her up on the offer, but both of the girls began to insist. Tringali, who had evidently drunk several beers, finally obliged them, jumping on stage and stripping to the music, taking off an item in response to each one the dancers removed. The players responded with hoots and cheers, a couple of them looking embarrassed and uncomfortable. Soon Tringali was stark naked and rotating his hips, his hands on the shoulders of one of the girls, who was now equally nude.

The players were enjoying the demonstration until loud sounds were heard from the club downstairs, and the girls, panicking, started grabbing their things and telling the boys to follow them to the back door. The backs of the clubs along the strip on the north side were carved into the bottom slope of Telegraph Hill, so the back door, despite being on the second floor, exited straight onto a narrow alley. Vince had a lot of items to put on and barely made it outside before the police came upstairs. They were met by Wendy at the door. Most of them knew and liked her, and almost all were either friends or had, in a small way, a financial interest in the club not being harassed. She told them that they might not want to catch the kids who had just left. The squad took the hint and started making noise rummaging around the upstairs room, then proceeded back down the stairs.

For Vince it was just a matter of joining the other players running down the back alley and making their way back to the Hilltop. The team lived in fear from that evening on that Kuharich would find out about their escapade. I never did learn if he had or not, but the way the team walked on eggshells for the next few weeks must have given him cause to wonder.

We came home from New York to face the San Diego Naval Training Center. Like the Camp Pendleton Marines, their team was filled with ex-college stars and drafted professionals. We were heavy favorites, playing on our home turf at Kezar and because of our dismantling of the Marines team, even though the Navy Blue Jackets had previously won over Loyola. It went as expected, with USF winning 26 to 7. It would have been just another win over what was considered an inferior military team if it weren't for something only the most observant fan would have noticed. I did, only because I was so used to watching Ollie run and seeing our players flatten the defenders before they could reach Ollie. It was subtle, but after the first quarter, Ollie started to look for contact. Twice during the second and third quarters, some Navy players had to be carried off the field, and another was helped off never to return to the game. I was curious as to what had caused Ollie to go from avoiding hits to punishing the men trying to tackle him. So, the next morning, while Scrap Iron was seeing to the bumps, bruises, scrapes, and strains, I asked Ollie and Scudero what was up. I knew Kuharich wasn't happy with Matson putting himself at risk of injury and had talked to his player. I thought I would go to the source, but I got nothing from Ollie, who just told me he hadn't noticed any difference. Scudero and later Bob St. Clair gave me a full account. A number of the Navy players were talking trash. This was normal, but their remarks were racist and went far beyond decency.

The first Blue Jacket had been carried off after an offensive play in which Ollie had simply turned into the defender, knocking him down and then running over his body and head. The second time the Blue Jacket linebacker had managed to grab hold of Ollie's waist, the type of tackle I had seen Ollie shed at least two dozen times earlier in the season, but this time he hit the man with a stiff arm that was more a punch than anything else. They both went down to the ground with the tackler's head between Ollie's elbow and the ground. The guy was knocked out and they took him off the field on a stretcher. Five minutes later he was on his feet on the sideline, but he never reentered the game.

The third time was another offensive play in which Ollie took the handoff from Brown, faked right, and cut left. The Blue Jacket tackle, an All-Southwest Conference selection from the University of Texas named Ken Jackson, had a clear shot at Ollie. The guy was listed in the program at 240 pounds, but he looked like Navy food agreed with him. He was fast and had a good angle on Ollie, and even in the press box he could be heard screaming. He outweighed Ollie by at least 40, maybe as many as 50, pounds. Two steps away from the inevitable, Ollie switched the ball to the outside and stuck his right hand out to try to stiff-arm the man, at least to lessen the impact. It never came. Just as the defender reached for Matson, Gino Marchetti hit him from the side. As fast as the Navy man was approaching Ollie, Marchetti was moving faster. The collision was epic. Marchetti lifted the man completely off his feet, his momentum carrying them almost five yards before they hit the ground, Marchetti grinding over the body beneath him as they skidded to a stop. Marchetti stood up and yelled something at the prostrate, unmoving man, turned his back, and walked to the sideline.

Scudero was still fired up the next day when I met with him and Bob St. Clair. Scooter was usually vocal enough for two or three players, but today St. Clair took the lead.

"You couldn't hear that shit they were saying to Ollie? The refs weren't doing anything about it. This isn't the south, even though a lot of those assholes were from there."

"We told Ollie in the huddle," chimed in Scudero, "that we were going to take care of them even if it got us thrown outta the damn game. I mean, they were calling him coon, Tar Baby, and monkey."

"Ollie just told us to slow down. He said, 'I can take care of it myself,'" continued St. Clair. "And boy, did he. Did you see the first guy he hit wander off the field to our sideline before they turned him around?"

Scudero blew snot from his broken nose and said with a cackle, "Did you hear Gino when he blew that guy up? Good thing the line judge hadn't arrived. He pointed to him and said, 'Who's the coon now?' Burl and I were the only ones close enough, I guess. It was the first time I ever saw Burl smile on the field."

"Tringali got some revenge too, but I guess you saw that, huh, Pete?"

I told him that I had seen Vince get called for two penalties, one of them after the play was over, and asked if that was part of it.

St. Clair just laughed in his deep voice and told me, "Oh yeah. Tringali went a little nuts out there. He kicked a guy in the balls and yelled at him, 'And I'm a ginni. How does that feel?' That was his second unnecessary roughness call. I'm surprised they didn't kick him out of the game."

Later that day I asked Bud Kerr, the line coach, if the coaches had heard the comments on the sideline. He said they had and were worried that it would take the team out of the game plan. When Tringali started hitting people, Coach Kuharich said that since Vince was always a little crazy, no one would notice. Kerr said the coach was very happy when Ollie took things into his own hands, that it was hard to call a penalty on the man who had the ball. Then it was time to plan the next day's practice and prepare for the seventh game of the season against rival Santa Clara.

We were favored by thirteen points against Santa Clara, even though they had beaten us the year before quite convincingly. Coach Kuharich fired up the troops on the first day of practice. He thought he saw the first sign that being 6 and 0, and destroying the opposition each time, was breeding complacency. He yelled at the team as if we were 0 and 6, his voice rising in pitch throughout the week. It didn't seem possible, but he worked the team harder than any week before, except perhaps the second week when he had built team comradery.

In the first game against San Jose, we had attracted only 5,000 or so fans. At Fordham there were upwards of ten times as many spectators. I guess my constant reminders to the city's sportswriters about our record and our players were doing some good. There was also the growing rumor that USF was likely to be offered a bowl game to keep the program going financially.

The college football season provided a lot of copy for the sports page. Whatever the reason, I didn't have to work so hard that week. The papers were coming to me for material rather than my having to force it on them. On Friday, the headline of the Sporting Green of the *Chronicle* touted a POSSIBLE SELL-OUT AT KEZAR. As it was, over 37,000 fans saw us beat Santa Clara 26 - 7. Matson had another two touchdowns, leading the Dons' ground game to a total 321 yards while giving up minus 18 to the Broncos. Marchetti and Toler were beasts, while St. Clair and Thomas let nothing around their end.

Ralph Thomas and St. Clair were a sight to see standing next to each other in their defensive stances. St. Clair was in his junior year and edging over 6' 8", a lot of it legs. In a three-point stance, his butt stuck up, giving him the raked look of a Carlsbad skunk. Thomas was much smaller at just 5' 11" and 185 pounds, but there wasn't a tougher man on the field. His toughness had been honed by his position as the eleventh kid in a fifteen-child family. Four of his siblings were older brothers. His was a strict Catholic upbringing with competition encouraged among the brothers and sisters but also an insistence on strong family unity. He was the first person in the family to go to college. He ended up playing for Kuharich for seven years, all four of his years at USF and three in the pros. When he played professionally for Kuharich with the Cardinals, the coach sat next to him on one of the trips and confided in him that he was the source of his single greatest disappointment while he coached at USF – that he would have sent him away without a scholarship except he had already invested in his train ticket. It seems that Scrap Iron had come to his office and said that he had found this great farm boy from Wisconsin, 6' 2" and 210 pounds. When Ralph walked into his office for the first time and stood in front of the desk at just under 5' 11" and 175 pounds with clothes on, he'd felt like breaking Scrap Iron's nose back to straight.

The Santa Clara game might have been Thomas's best overall game. Santa Clara kept trying to run inside. St. Clair appeared to give them the opportunity by shading toward the outside, but every play that cut inside the end found Thomas waiting for the running back, the blocking scheme destroyed and St. Clair ready with a smile to clean up anything Thomas had left unfinished.

It was the earliest the band had started playing "Goodnight Irene" at any previous home game, and the USF fans went home happy and hoarse.

CHAPTER TWENTY-ONE

"I know I've said it before, and it was true then, but this is the most important game of the season." Those were the first words out of Coach Kuharich's mouth at Monday's practice. We had no more home games at Kezar left. The College of the Pacific game was in Stockton at the Pacific Memorial stadium. Then, if we were still undefeated, we had our last scheduled game against Loyola in the Pasadena Rose Bowl. The Pacific game was to have a late start at 8:00 pm, and Kuharich thought it was an advantage to his team as they wouldn't have to worry about a hot afternoon, which was always a possibility in the Central Valley.

I could tell that Kuharich was worried about this game. Pacific was a good team and was being talked about for a post-season bowl game bid as well. They also had a potential All-American in Eddie Macon, a running back with numbers almost as strong as Matson's. This was a game the papers thought was almost as important as the Big Game between Cal and Stanford in establishing the credibility of west coast football. The weekend of our last game against Loyola, Stanford would have a chance to clinch their claim to a Rose Bowl spot by beating Cal. Kuharich was also glad that his team had gotten used to playing in front of large crowds. The papers estimated that there would be over 40,000 spectators at Stockton, and this time they wouldn't be a home crowd, even though there was a large contingency of San Franciscans who would caravan the two-hour drive to Stockton.

I was becoming a fan. It was not just the 7 and 0 record; I was genuinely fond of the players. Maybe it was because I had written so much about them—not only about their performances, but also about their personalities and more recently their character. I was looking forward to watching the game. Kuharich still showed his bias toward ball control, practicing some running plays featuring Scudero that had been in the playbook all season but not yet used. Then, on Thursday, with only a light practice left, he gave the team a real twist for the offense. He drew up and practiced a single-wing scheme they had never seen, not even in training camp. The backfield and offensive line were so connected that they took to the new formation easily, and after two repetitions they looked like they had been running it all season.

In the Sunday *Chronicle* the day after the game, the headline ran USF AND MATSON SWARM OVER COP. However, Dick Friendlich, the reporter writing the account under the headline, thought the loss was due more to Tiger miscues than to the Dons' good play. Four minutes into the second quarter, USF was up 20 to 0. It was true that the Dons' offense had only as many first downs—three—as they had touchdowns, but a lot of that was due to the defense, as Gino Marchetti harassed the COP player sent back to the end zone to receive Ed Brown's punt, then fell on it for the first touchdown. The second touchdown came as halfback Macon tried to elude a defender near the ten-yard line and lost the ball, which was recovered by the Dons' Ralph Thomas. The next play saw Brown pass to Bob St. Clair, who scored, carrying Macon, now on defense, with him for the second score. The third saw Burl Toler leading the entire left side of the line into the COP backfield, blocking a punt which went high in the air and was recovered in the end zone by Mike Mergen playing right tackle. Kuharich tried a pass to Scudero for the extra point, but it was badly thrown by Brown and they led 20 rather than 21 to 0.

COP got back in the game when Matson fumbled on the 25-yard line, and four plays later the Tigers punched it over from the 2-yard line to close the half at 20 to 7. The feeling of being back in the game lasted through the third quarter, in which defensive line play controlled the momentum for both squads. But any hope the Pacific team had that they could overcome the 13-point deficit was quickly dispelled when Matson broke to the outside for a 68-yard touchdown run to make the score 27 to 7.

I'm not sure if COP let up, or if it was the single wing that Kuharich now decided to insert, but the next three scores were all Brown. First he launched a deep end zone pass to Merrill Peacock for another seven. Then, after stopping COP with a Matson interception, Brown found St. Clair at right end and he dragged two defenders with him across the goal line. In the last seconds of the game, the Dons again had the ball. Brown went back to pass, but all his targets were well covered, so he tucked the ball under his right arm and sprinted for the final score.

47 to 14 would seem like a blowout, and in a way it was, particularly in the fourth quarter, but if you just looked at the stats, you might wonder how the Dons had won the game. COP had slightly more overall yardage; they had 18 first downs to USF's 7. They even had twice as many pass completions. They had the distinction of scoring the first and only rushing touchdown on the Dons for the whole season. What they didn't have was Matson, who was outstanding on both sides of the ball, or Marchetti and Toler playing like a stone wall on defense along with the hulking St. Clair and Thomas on the other side of the line. We had now won eight straight games and were ranked eighth in the nation.

After the win, the papers were full of speculation concerning an Orange Bowl bid. Van C. Kussrow, the chairman of the Orange Bowl committee, and another board member were quoted as saying that USF had improved its position as to a bid. They both said that they would prefer a representative from the west coast to meet Georgia Tech, which had already been selected for one of the spots. The board, however, had put off selecting the second team because of the logjam at the top of the Southwest Conference, where Baylor, TCU, Oklahoma, and Rice were all being considered. As it turned out, the four southern teams had a shared advantage over Kuharich's Dons going into the last game of the season. I shot off word to all the east coast guys I knew, including Grantland, that the day that we beat Pacific so convincingly, Fordham defeated Temple 35 to 6.

Kuharich was glad of the extra day they would have between games, since they would play Loyola on Sunday, November 25th— Thanksgiving weekend. Many of his players showed the effects of their hard hitting in the Pacific game. Chief among those injured was Matson, who had bruised ribs which, thankfully, X-rays showed not to be broken or cracked. The same was true for Gino's ankle and Scudero's right heel.

I had not had so much to write about since the Fordham game. There were so many stories besides the outcome of the game. Ollie only needed 118 yards to break the all-time college rushing record, and if he scored three touchdowns, he would own that single-season mark as well. Loyola was not without its incentive, either. Don Klosterman, Loyola's quarterback, would almost certainly surmount the previous college record for passing yardage. USF led the nation in run defense, so we were sure to see a massive amount of Klosterman.

Unfortunately, most of what I wrote went for naught, as we played on Sunday in Pasadena, and Saturday saw Stanford take on Cal at the Farm. Still, I talked to Darrell Wilson at the *Chronicle* and got him to put a piece in Saturday's paper, an amazing feat since the first five pages of the Sporting Green would be filled with every conceivable story and statistic about the Big Game. All the writers praised the favored Stanford Indians, which shows you what newspaper guys know, because Cal destroyed the Big Red

Machine in front of 95,000 fans. Still, Darrell got in a short piece saying that the Dons were an undefeated 8 – 0 squad that would be favored to beat Loyola nine times out of ten, and they were being considered for a major bowl. Then, probably because he was irritated that I had bugged him so much, he mentioned the loss to LMU the previous year when the Lions came back to beat us after we led 28 – 13 in the second half. My bad timing held on as the next day the papers were again filled with Cal – Stanford and the amazing underdog win of the Bears.

It was ironic, as the team got ready to play the most important game of the season, one that could determine a bowl bid and ensure a future for football at USF, that Earl James McGrath, the United States Commissioner of Education, announced some statistics. There was a 7.8% drop in college enrollment in the fall of 1951, with male enrollment declining 10.8%, and most damaging for USF, male freshman enrollment had seen a reduction of 12.3%. I thought it likely, because USF was an all-male institution and because of veiled comments by Fathers Dunne and Feeley, that the University of San Francisco had suffered a greater decrease. I could spend a whole tape talking about the things that went along with the education you received at USF. The attention to morality and service to the community—these were woven into the fabric of any course taught at USF. I didn't take Chemistry, but I suspect that somehow Jesuit values made up a part of that curriculum as well. It makes sense that any young man who had the morality and conviction to choose a Jesuit school would also be more likely to enlist for the Korean War, decreasing the enrollment figures even more.

Kuharich gave the team the gift of a Monday off. It was the first time in the season that we had two consecutive days off and one wasn't used for traveling. Kuharich also secured Kezar for practice sessions on Tuesday, Wednesday, and Thursday. Friday was not possible as the San Francisco Polytechnic High School game would be held that weekend to a full house. Our home practice field was so chewed up that it wouldn't be available for baseball season in the spring if we ground on it much more. I suspect that Kuharich was also unhappy about the small crowds that had started showing up at practices. They lined the wire fence that surrounded the field and watched from the hill to the west, which looked down on the players. Coach Kerr confirmed my suspicions and told me that was why the week before he had dismissed the team, then called them back after the spectators left to install the single wing that we had used at Stockton. Kezar was a true stadium and we could control the access.

Each day at 1 pm, we would walk down the hill through Golden Gate Park to the stadium. It was strange not having the band following us, blaring out our fight song, with the fans walking behind as we went through the greenery. At 3 pm we would turn the field over to Poly High School, the team that St. Clair had played for as a teenager.

Golden Gate Park is a marvel. It is a third larger than Central Park here in New York and contains more things to do. I spent many days rowing around Stow Lake, which was less than a mile from our campus. The ocean end of the park allowed free viewing of world-class polo matches from blankets laid just beyond the boards. Both provided for cheap dates. There was even a bison paddock three times the size of a football field, containing a dozen of the beasts, all female. The park was conceived in 1871 far to the west of the residential part of the city. It ran from the Pacific Ocean through sculpted sand dunes three miles from the beach toward the developed part of town. It's huge, three-and-a-half miles from the water to where USF stands in the exact center of the city. It is a half-mile wide from north to south. Landscape architect and gardener John McLaren, a Scot, is generally given credit for transforming the 1017 acres of sand into a green, sylvan setting for museums, athletic fields, and secluded glades.

McLaren did this by tapping the giant aquifer of fresh water that lies beneath the city's oceanfront and by building two great windmills adjacent to the ocean. These pumped the water up through the length of the park and then down by gravity back to the beach. I loved the park, and even though we only zig-zagged through the eastern end, I felt the team drew strength from their passage through peaceful glens and nooks on dirt trails on their way to the athletic equivalent of armed combat.

In Kezar, watching the team practice, I was aware of how the season had changed not only the team—as individuals and as a group—but also the coaches. Kuharich was still referred to as the Barracuda by the players, his voice was still shrill and his instructions blunt, but now there was a sense of respect in his tone. He had become more of a teacher than a disciplinarian. He had driven the players ruthlessly the year before and in the beginning of the '51 season, but as he saw the players respond and perform up to and sometimes beyond his expectations, his approach changed. When he saw a mistake, he still yelled, but often with a smile or a remark at the end that would make the team laugh. The miscreant was still chastised, but the teasing of his comrades ensured just as effectively as had the head coach's wrath that the missed assignment or mistake would not be repeated.

Kuharich's staff was now joined full time by freshman coach Brad Lynn, and they worked in perfect harmony. Individually they still coached their positions, but by now they knew where every man on the field should be on a certain play, not just their group. Their players were part of a collective, not individual pieces. The team had changed as well. There was a sense of group confidence that touched every player, from the starters to the third string. It was hard to notice the change from game to game. But when one remembered the first game against San Jose State and Kuharich's disgust over the individual play he saw in that win, then the team play and obvious concern for one another of the last few contests showed that the change had been significant. You had only to watch Scudero to be impressed at how the individuals of the team had come together as a single entity. Scooter was not only not jealous of Matson's workload or the fact that downfield he was Ollie's lead blocker, he seemed to take particular pleasure when Ollie came back after a play had ended and slapped him on the ass for clearing the path. Even the giant St. Clair, who had been used to being the main focus when he was at Poly High School, had accepted being just a piece of the whole, an important piece, but with the knowledge that he needed to help others and have others help him in order to have the greatest success. The players showed a sense of total confidence that they had become something great and could beat any opponent.

I watched them scrimmage, Ollie tucking the balls only under his left arm because of his sore ribs, Scudero with massive amounts of tape, applied by Scrap Iron, holding a huge piece of foam rubber against his injured heel. Gino did not practice, his right ankle looking twice the size of the left from swelling and Scrap Iron's tape. All of them had demanded of the coach not to be held out of practice. Only Gino was denied, and he spent as much energy walking the sidelines at the side of Coach Kerr as did the players running on the field. I almost felt sorry for LMU and Georgia Tech.

CHAPTER TWENTY-TWO

We were going to take the bus from the campus to the train station to board the express to Los Angeles. Kuharich had decided to take the morning train, which would cost more money as they would have to take rooms in a hotel Friday night and take the evening train back after the game on Sunday. A consideration was that the players would have to gather at 7 am. This would not be a problem for those staying in the barracks, but for those living across the city it met an early wake-up, particularly if they had to take public transportation.

Chief among those players was Bob St. Clair, who lived far out on Capitol off of Ocean Avenue in the Ingleside district of San Francisco. His house was only a mile from where Joe Scudero lived in the outer Mission district, but they never met until they played high school football against one another. This was undoubtedly a good thing, as St. Clair had a similar rap sheet with the police as Scudero. Both had been arrested numerous times for fighting. Both were considered slightly nuts. At fourteen years old, St. Clair was only 5'9" and 150 pounds and at the time belonged to a gang. While at a party, a rival gang beat him up, cracking some ribs, chipping a tooth, and breaking his nose. During the next year, he grew six inches and put on 60 pounds. Now fifteen, he found one of his attackers at a soda fountain. The kid didn't recognize St. Clair as the fourteen-year-old he had held while others beat him up the year before, but this didn't stop

St. Clair from breaking his nose and loosening a tooth. Learning where the other gang leader lived, St. Clair went to the door and politely asked the kid's mother if her son was in. When the kid came to the door, St. Clair swung on him, knocking him down and then following him down the hallway hitting him while his mother screamed. It was a minor miracle that after a couple years at USF, he and Scudero became good friends.

St. Clair used to ride his bike west on Ocean to 19th Avenue. In the early forties, much of the area west of 19th was still sand dunes or vegetable farms. St. Clair would jump the fence and grab vegetables, then ride his bike away. One day as he jumped the fence, he got a shotgun full of rock salt in his backside, which his sister had to remove. It was the end of his stealing vegetables. When he entered Polytechnic High School, his family moved further west down Ocean to near Aptos Junior High School. It was closer to Polytechnic and the University of San Francisco, which are separated by less than half a mile of Golden Gate Park and Kezar Stadium, but he still had to transfer from streetcar to bus three times before arriving at either school.

The war had provided a great opportunity for builders just to the west of St. Clair's neighborhood; they leveled the sand dunes and placed houses, sides touching, filling over 4,500 acres. The construction was so rapid that some weeks they completed and sold twenty houses a day. Before 1935, there were only a few rows of houses near the beach south of Golden Gate Park. By 1950 there were only a few square blocks of dunes left. The city had given Spanish names to the streets that ran from east to west in what was called the Sunset District in recognition of San Francisco's Spanish heritage prior to the Gold Rush of 1849. In 1935 there was only one street that meandered through the dunes. This became 19th Avenue. In just fifteen years, the rest of the area became a checkerboard of rectangular blocks crowded with houses, twelve blocks to the mile.

———

Kuharich came out of his office as the players gathered at the Fulton Street gate. He was smiling, which was odd enough in itself. He moved to where his coaches were grouped, with only Scrap Iron missing, as he was checking the luggage that contained the team equipment and the training supplies, mostly iodine and roll after roll of adhesive tape.

"I just got off the phone," he said, making sure the players could not hear him. He waited for his coaches to ask about the call; none did, and I knew better than to say anything.

"I got the call," continued Kuharich. "We are on the list. The Orange Bowl is sending a couple of representatives to watch the Loyola game. This is it. We win big and we go to Miami."

The usually stoical Bud Kerr gave a hoot, and Brad Lynn clapped him on the back. I of course was ecstatic. The game in New York had been my first chance to make my mark, and this was the next. I noticed the players looking at us. I knew that before we loaded on the train, the news would be out. It might even have come from me, as I was almost jumping up and down. The Orange Bowl was the Holy Grail. I knew that Georgia Tech, the number one team in the nation in at least one poll, had already accepted a bid. A win would in all probability give the Dons a national title. Even more important, it would save the program for the foreseeable future. The coach had told Father Feeley and President Dunne prior to his meeting with the coaches. As the excited players milled around the quad, the two administrators exited the Jesuit residence with two small overnight cases in hand. They would be joining us in Pasadena.

I was supposed to monitor the players as they studied as well as proctor three tests during the train ride. Study hall was a joke, but I could get the seven players who were taking the tests into one end of the dining car. Two professors had trusted me, or more likely Coach Kuharich, to be honest and supervise fairly. One of the students was Burl Toler. I placed him at the rear door to the compartment and I took the front. Burl's stare over his wire-rimmed glasses kept his teammates in line far more effectively than my presence did. Each test was given an hour, but only Gino and Toler took the full hour—Gino because he needed every minute, and Toler because he must have checked each question a dozen times.

The rest of the trip was filled with talk of the Orange Bowl. The team to a man believed that a win over Loyola would make it impossible for the Orange Bowl Board not to give them the invite. At 1 pm, Coach Kuharich called all the players into a single passenger car. If there was any doubt as to who the starters were going to be, you could tell by which ones were sitting in the seats. The others sat on the floor. The coach gave verbal instructions on how to deal with the Loyola passing game and Klosterman's tendencies. He had gone over this information numerous times during film study and practice, but this time with the rocking of the train and the confined quarters, it was more dramatic.

Watching the team practice the last few days in Kezar, and listening intently to Kuharich as the train lurched down the track, clacking at precise intervals, I was again reminded of how the team dynamic had changed. St. Clair and Scudero were sitting next to each other, listening to the coach's last instructions. The first time I had seen them together two years ago, I was sure there was going to be a fight. Scudero was known never to back down and to love a fight, and St. Clair was as mean and tough as he was big. He outweighed the running back by at least 70 pounds.

I don't know when the transformation took place, but it did, without either of them losing his hyper-aggressive character. I remember that in the second San Jose State game, our fourth of the season, St. Clair's number had been called for a fly pattern down the right sideline. The play stuck in my mind because we didn't pass much that game. I think we had only five yards total in the air. St. Clair was being covered by a linebacker who had stopped his forward progress and was holding him upright for the San Jose safety, who was coming up hard and low, going for his knees. From across the field, from where he had been running his own route, flew Scudero. Both Scooter and the San Jose safety left their feet at the same time, but Scudero did it with more force and speed. His 150 pounds hit the defender, shoulder to helmet. The man flew sidewise, landing in a heap without touching St. Clair. Scudero popped up, pointing briefly at his teammate before returning to the huddle as the whistle blew. San Jose State had to help the safety off the field, so there was a time out. As St. Clair moved back to the huddle, I saw him pat Scudero on the head and nod his own. It didn't look like either of them said anything, and I didn't hear anything either that day or after, but their relationship seemed to change at that point. As the season went on, they spent more and more time together, including studying the new pass schemes that Kuharich put in with the single wing. Kuharich understood that the other coaches would know of his propensity to control the game by relying on the running game. The single wing formation was particularly a running formation. With Brown an accomplished running threat, the defense would have to flow toward the side the play was going. Halfway to scrimmage, the coach had Brown stop and rifle a pass to the vacated opposite side linebacker position. Going left, St. Clair would receive; going right, Peacock caught the pass. If the linebackers didn't commit to the run, then Brown would keep it or lateral to either Scudero or Matson. Only Brown's great athletic ability and strong arm made the play possible. It was almost unfair.

Scudero and St. Clair were not the only example of the team coming together. Marchetti had become a quiet leader. If an opposing lineman was eye-gouging or going after knees with crack back blocks on offense, the team told Gino, and the dirty stuff stopped or the player was helped from the field. Sometimes it involved a penalty on Marchetti, and once or twice retaliation was attempted, but never with a satisfactory result. Gino watched over his own side of the line, Tringali next to him and Toler behind. As far as I could tell, the coaches were correct. Tringali was just nuts. He was undersized for an internal lineman, but he made up for it with an intensity that bordered on derangement. He was the point of the opponents' blocking schemes because no one wanted to waste time or energy running at Marchetti or Toler. For his part, Tringali began to understand Gino's friendship and protection, and perhaps because of their shared Italian heritage, he would act with bravado after a play, knowing that his brother—his much bigger and tougher brother—was just behind him.

If Marchetti had a connection with Tringali because of the Italian thing, he had no shared heritage with Burl Toler. Yet on the field, in team meetings, while traveling, and at meals, the two were inseparable. After their very first game together, I could tell that they worked in harmony, carrying out Coach Bud Kerr's defensive plans but also putting in their own wrinkles. I remember asking Coach Kerr about it sometime around mid-season. He just grinned and said his defense was drawn up for mortal individuals, not for Toler and Marchetti. Those two were bigger, faster, and smarter than any players he had ever coached. He said they played like they had two giant bodies with one head. Tringali took advantage of the two being next to him and behind him. If Gino was being blocked to the inside, Burl would automatically be on his right shoulder, and what was more important, Gino knew he would be there, giving Tringali a smaller area to cover. I know that outside class, Toler helped Marchetti with his studies. Then there was the classroom confrontation with Father Giambastiani, which got back to me through both Father Feeley and Pierre Salinger, who was observing the class. That was Pierre, always in the right place at the right time.

Rozelle rang for his assistant. Seconds later she opened the door with a steno pad and pen in hand. "Jeanie, would you please have the deli send up some sandwiches for us? Italian and Swiss on a hard roll for Jim, and pastrami and Swiss with sauerkraut for me. Order yourself something as well." That done, he turned to the tape recorder, which had only about 20% of the reel left, and replaced it with a fresh one. As he started it, he recited into the microphone, "'51 USF Dons, third reel." He stopped the machine and spoke to Jim Kensil. "Talking this much makes me dry. You want a beer? It's almost noon. The sandwiches will be here in a half hour."

He got a nod from Kensil, who got up from the sofa, stretched, and moved to the wall bar, pulling two beers from the built-in refrigerator, opening them and giving one to his boss.

"This is a great story," said Rozelle, "but some of it I wouldn't print. I have a couple stories like that that I'll share on this tape; some are more private than others. But by the time anyone listens to this, sensibilities will have changed. This one might just be embarrassing to Gino, but if I know Gino, he'll just smile his lopsided grin and shrug his shoulders." Rozelle leaned over and clicked a toggle switch, and the reels began to turn.

We had this great priest, Father Giambastiani. He was a real character and a rabid sports fan. Basketball was his main love. He would always sit in the south upper deck seats and he'd be surrounded by students and athletes from different sports. Everybody loved him. He liked football too, but I always thought it was interesting that he preferred the round ball, probably because of his size. He was almost as tall as Gino but nowhere near as heavy. Always wearing a smile, he had a tremendous vitality. He ruled his classroom with an iron fist, which was interesting because he also made his classes fun. For no reason at all, he would slip into a perfect impersonation of Benito Mussolini, Il Duce, eliciting laughter from his class while getting the message of that day's lesson over in a way that stuck in the minds of his students.

We had arrived back at school from the Fordham game and Gino had not slept on the plane, preferring to play cards with Ed Brown and Vince Tringali. The next morning, he told Vince and Burl that he was going to sleep in, and they would have to do without him in class. I told you that USF was a stickler for grades; well, Father Giambastiani was a strict adherent to that doctrine. That morning, taking attendance, he called "Marchetti!" Getting no answer, he repeated, "Gino John Marchetti!" Still receiving no response and noticing the empty seat near the back, Giambastiani turned to Scudero and asked where Marchetti was. Scudero, being wiser than most around the Jesuit priests, said that he didn't know—that he hadn't seen him since the previous evening. St. Clair, not getting what was happening, volunteered that he thought Gino was still asleep and that he hadn't been able to sleep on the way back from the game on the east coast. He received looks that could kill from both Scudero and Toler but remained oblivious.

Giambastiani told the class to stay put, he would be back in a few minutes, and barreled out of the classroom, robes flying, heading to the athletic dorm. He quickly found Marchetti sleeping in bed, grabbed his ear, and twisted. Gino came awake immediately and started to swing on the priest, who twisted harder and moved deftly to one side. Maintaining his grip, he pulled Gino back to the classroom, barefoot, with only his T-shirt and a pair of shorts on, and deposited him in the first row. Then, once Gino was seated, without hesitation, he continued the roll call, calling out, "Gino John Marchetti!" For seconds the class did not know how to react; then one person laughed, and the top was off. Father Giambastiani didn't seem to mind, but Marchetti turned as red as his right ear.

We arrived in Pasadena after transferring trains in Los Angeles just after five pm. The team was ravenous after being subjected to a breakfast and lunch of train food. Kuharich took us to an Italian family restaurant that was half a block from the hotel, which reminded us of the one in Corning. Tringali said the food was nowhere near as good as what you got in North Beach, but it didn't stop Marchetti from having seconds and thirds of the ravioli.

The coaches and I sat apart from the squad. Fathers Dunne, Feeley, and Giambastiani, who had joined the team at the train station, sweating and huffing as the cab dropped him off just as the team was going to board, ate with the players.

Uncharacteristically, Coach Kuharich looked at each of us and said, "We'll have a short meeting in my room right after dinner. Think hard! Is there anything we've forgotten?"

Bud Kerr, who was senior among the coaches, took the responsibility of answering. "Coach, you've done everything possible. There might be some surprises they'll throw at us during the game that we'll have to adjust to, but you've done your job. The team is ready. We should win by three touchdowns."

All the coaches voiced their agreement. I even felt the need to speak up, expressing my opinion that the team could not be in a better mood. Kuharich would have none of it and still looked worried as he plowed through an apple cobbler. The meeting at the motel was more of the same. I thought the coaches would sleep soundly, but not Kuharich. I was also concerned—not about the team or the outcome of the game, despite Loyola having the home-field advantage and the leading passer in the nation in Klosterman. I was worried about finding the Orange Bowl representatives before the game and sitting next to them. I would expect them to be in the press box, but if they chose to watch from the stands, I would have my job cut out for me finding them.

CHAPTER
TWENTY-THREE

In the six months I had been working as the football team's publicity director, I had been hearing about the great stadium at Notre Dame. As I've mentioned before, it wasn't only Kuharich who had the Notre Dame connection; Bud Kerr and Scrap Iron both were Notre Dame alumni and even the freshman coach, who was full time with the varsity squad now that the freshman season was over, had transferred to and graduated from the famous football school. Now, walking with the team onto the field of the Rose Bowl, I felt awe. Notre Dame sat 62,000 but it looked as though the home of the Golden Dome could fit inside the Rose Bowl. The Pasadena stadium held 104,000. The press box and private boxes were fifty steps up the west side from the field level and three stories high. It would be almost impossible to find the representatives from the Orange Bowl if they didn't go to the press box or the box that Father Dunne had reserved for himself and Father Feeley.

I watched the players looking around the overwhelming enclosure and was glad that the thirty thousand primarily LMU fans would look insignificant, their cheers lost in the expanse. Still, the players for the most part looked intimidated. I couldn't help being a wise guy, more than anything to break the tension that showed on the players' faces.

"Not nearly as big as Notre Dame's, huh Coach?" I yelled back to Coach Kuharich, who was walking behind the players.

"Oh, nothing could be as big as Notre Dame," yelled Tringali, and the whole team cracked up. No more tension. Even the coaching staff laughed. The coach tried to keep his look stern, but he couldn't do it. The joke was on him and he joined in laughing.

"We'll just have to build in the end zone with seats," he yelled back. "At least the Golden Dome sells out every game!"

"But they wouldn't play us, Coach," replied Tringali, and this time Kuharich's laugh had an edge to it.

After a quick walk around the field, Kuharich led the team into the locker room. I excused myself and walked past the fifty rows of seats, up the hundred steps to the enclosed structure sitting on top of the stadium rim. I found the press box and the USF box just underneath it on the level below. Neither Father Dunne nor Father Feeley was there. The team had taken the bus from the hotel without them since we were arriving three hours prior to the game and an hour and a half before the gates opened. Only Father Giambastiani had bused in with the team and coaches, and with his tall frame he almost seemed part of the squad, though he was careful to remain apart. It was easier going down the stadium stairs than up them. I knew there must have been an elevator somewhere, but the lockers were on the other end of the field and I was too amped up to search for it.

The locker room was a scene of quiet confidence, with players stretching, getting taped, disrobing, and putting their things in the provided lockers. Gino Marchetti sat on the bench in front of his locker, his shoulders hunched, his head hanging, his great callused hands holding up his drooping head. Toler took the locker next to him, looking at the dejected figure as he started putting his things in the locker.

"What's up, Gino? You look like your dog died."

"Scrap Iron and the doc won't clear me. I can't put any pressure on the outside of my ankle. I'm not playing."

"Can't we get them to change their minds? I could try and talk to them."

"Nah, they're right. Loyola would go after me after the first couple of plays showed that I couldn't move. I wouldn't be able to put any pressure on Klosterman. I couldn't help and I'd probably hurt the team. I'm going to suit up, though. It'll make me feel like I'm still part of the team at least."

"Big guy, you're the reason we're here. You know how many running yards teams have made over our side all season? Minus 12 yards the whole season is all. The whole season! You just get well for the bowl game. Hillig has been playing backup for you all season. When you've taken a breather, he did okay. I'll watch out for him. Jay will do fine."

The team went onto the field and warmed up. It was a beautiful day, just under 70 degrees, and thankfully there was no smog, that noxious blend of fog and smoke that Herb Caen, who was as much a fixture in San Francisco as Grantland Rice was in New York, had christened the specific type of air pollution that frequented the Los Angeles Basin. It burned the eyes and irritated the lungs to the point that you had trouble breathing. It had been a minor irritant when I lived in Los Angeles growing up before the war, settling in maybe two or three times a summer. But since the war it had increased tenfold, and each year it had gotten worse. Pasadena was not immune, especially if the wind was off shore. That day was clear, however, with no sign of the yellow-brown haze.

Our practice went as expected; the team was sharp and confident. Brown's passes were accurate and he even kicked the ball well. The rest of the team moved at half speed, flexing and stretching their muscles, getting the blood flowing, and after twenty minutes we returned to the locker room, where Gino immediately went to Scrap Iron with his shoes and socks off and asked to be taped. His adrenaline had kicked in watching the team warm up and he was no longer gloomy. Scrap Iron just shook his head and complied, double-taping Marchetti's right ankle so that it would hardly fit in his cleats. Then he took an additional turn of tape around the outside of the shoe and halfway up his calf. When he was done he said, "You still ain't playing!"

It was getting close to game time and I was genuinely starting to worry about how I was going to find the Orange Bowl representatives. I needn't have worried, though. Father Giambastiani was just getting helped up on the bench at the front of the locker room to give the blessing when the door opened and a security guard stuck his head in. "Two men are here to see Father Dunne."

There was no mistaking the orange jackets visible behind the half-opened door. I hurried past Father Giambastiani as the two men opened the door fully, stepping past the guard, and moved into the room with an arrogance that came from knowing they held the fate of the team in their hands. The players, who had been joking around and starting to gather around Father Giambastiani, fell quiet, the orange sport coats with the large Orange Bowl insignias on the breast pockets putting an end to their gibes.

I moved quickly to them and introduced myself, giving my title. The men's names were Matthew Pratt and Webb Wood. Both shook my hand, but their attention was on the team, which was returning their interest in full. I went to Scrap Iron's stash of supplies and removed the small reel of film I had brought with me. I had been busy the week before splicing together pieces of footage from previous games, showing Brown completing pass after pass, Marchetti sacking quarterbacks and running backs alike, Toler and Scudero making play after play. I even had a couple of clips of St. Clair making a catch and trotting back to the huddle with Scudero at his side. It accentuated his height, making him look even more like a giant than he was.

The two men were still standing inside the door when I got back to them and gave them the reel box, explaining what it was. I told them I hoped they would like what they saw, both on the film and on the field, and I would now take them to Father Dunne's box. I went through the door, but I had to wait for them in the hall as they continued to watch the team for a few more seconds. As we walked up the steps, they asked me how big the crowd was going to be and how many of them would be from USF. I told them the truth, that the game would draw 16,000, but perhaps fudged a little about the 5,000 Dons fans who had traveled south for the game. I explained that Thanksgiving had prevented a lot of our fans from traveling, and that if it were a home game, where they could have their family gatherings and take in the game, they would come close to filling Kezar. I was just giving them the word that our best lineman, Gino Marchetti, would not be playing because of an ankle sprain that was a week away from healing, when we reached the level of USF's box. I opened the door and introduced the two men to Father Dunne and Father Feeley. There was a third person in the box with the priests, Mr. Harney, one of our big donor alums. After a few pleasantries and inquiries about their trip, Father Dunne asked me if I would find Mr. Harney a seat in the press box. Harney looked put out that he wasn't going to be part of the group, and I wasn't all that thrilled myself about being dismissed from the conversation that would make or break the season and the Dons' run to a bowl bid.

A floor up and two doors down, I introduced Harney to Art Rosenbaum and Darrell Wilson of the *Chronicle*, who had made the trip down for the newspaper, leaving Palo Alto soon after the Cal Bears had upset the favored Stanford squad on its home turf. This placated the rich alum somewhat. I apologized for leaving to rejoin the team. I often spent all game in the press box, but I was nervous about this game and afraid of acting like a rookie as I had with Grantland Rice—that, and if I wasn't going to be allowed to be with the Orange Bowl reps, I wanted to be on the sidelines at least for the first half.

The game went as advertised: the powerful running game of the Dons against the brilliant passing attack of Don Klosterman of Loyola. Klosterman ended up passing 47 times with 24 completions for 211 yards in the air, but while that sounds like excellent production, they were all short yardage throws and Loyola never seriously threatened to score. That was mostly because Matson, Scudero, Brown, and Peacock were roaming the defensive backfield like a cast of center fielders. The Loyola ends were never open, causing Klosterman to throw short and seldom chancing to throw deep.

Loyola's defense was unexpectedly strong, and from the first sequence of downs it was apparent that the loss of Marchetti was going to be felt. The Lions put two men on St. Clair and Peacock and used the other seven to stop Matson. The left tackle position was now handled by Moriarity, and Tringali kept the Loyola linemen from Brown, but they were unable to open holes for Matson as Gino routinely did. At times, Loyola even brought up one of the corners and presented an eight-man line, all to stop Ollie.

The first quarter was hard fought, with neither team scoring, but I never got the feeling that Loyola was in the contest. The second quarter proved I was right when the Dons went 77 yards in 13 plays, with Ollie going over from the six for his first touchdown. Then, three minutes later, with Matson resting his sore ribs after tackling an LMU running back for a loss, Dick Huxley ran 72 yards through the Loyola defense, which was apparently resting with Ollie on the sidelines. It was more than the total yardage Huxley had gained all season. The drive ended in a score when Brown threw to Ralph Thomas for a six-yard completion.

Loyola's only score was the result of not having Gino on the line. With Ed Brown punting from our own 10-yard line, Ernie Cheatham ran through our left tackle and blocked the punt, which bounced back into the end zone. Brown was amazingly quick for a 205-pound athlete, and he beat Cheatham to the ball, covering it for a two-point safety rather than allowing a Loyola touchdown.

The Dons put the game completely out of reach in the fourth quarter when they converted on fourth down and two yards to go on the 14-yard line. Ollie got four yards, and later in the series went over for his second touchdown.

I had gone back up to the press box after the second score, the third time I had climbed those damned stairs. Halfway up I watched Ollie gain another 36 yards on five carries. Harney was still sitting with the two reporters, but closer to the entrance was Coach Jim Ryan, who was relaying instructions down to Kuharich on the sidelines. I did the quick math and told him that Ollie only needed 38 more yards to break the all-time collegiate mark. Jim relayed the information, but Loyola must have had someone keeping track as well. With only four minutes left, Loyola, which had passed almost every down, started running end sweeps, keeping inbounds and trying to run out the clock. They had accepted they had no chance for a win but were determined to prevent Ollie from getting the record. They ran out of downs and had to punt, which gave the ball to the Dons on the 32. Ollie got 18 of the next 26 yards against an 8-man line, with three players following his every move.

Kuharich could easily have had Brown pass against this tactic, but he wanted Ollie to get the record as much as Loyola wanted to thwart him. Then disaster struck as a handoff between Brown and Ollie was fumbled at the 6-yard line and Loyola recovered. With Loyola possessing the ball, the inexplicable happened. Klosterman, who had been killing time with running plays, decided to pass the ball. Vince Tringali intercepted and was tackled on the Loyola 32. With less than a minute left, Ollie got 16 yards on four carries, but the clock ran out with Ollie just four yards short of the total yardage mark and one touchdown short of that mark as well. His 112 yards for the game was his lowest total for any game that season. Short four yards and one touchdown, he was not despondent, and neither was the team as the final gun went off to cement their undefeated season. There were only about a thousand USF fans in the stadium, but the last five minutes rang out with verse after verse of "Goodnight Irene." Each chorus sounded louder than the last. The Loyola crowd was quiet as the song filled the stadium.

I got to the President's Box just as the two representatives from the Orange Bowl were leaving. They walked by me with only a nod of recognition, still holding my highlight reel. Inside, Father Dunne was talking with Father Feeley, their heads bent toward each other as if whispering. Neither was smiling. To this day I don't know how I refrained from asking what had transpired with the two Orange Bowl reps, but I didn't, and they didn't offer. When Feeley finally looked up and saw me standing at the door, he just told me they would take a cab and meet us at the train station.

CHAPTER
TWENTY-FOUR

Kuharich had reserved two passenger cars for the team and arranged for a buffet to feed the players in the dining car after the regular passengers had eaten. They would have to wait an hour, but they would be able to eat all they wanted. The priests and the coaching staff had seats in a third car to the rear, including one for me, but I didn't think I would get anything from either Dunne or Feeley from the way they had boarded the train. I asked Father Giambastiani, and he whispered that no decision had been reached. Giambastiani would be a good interview if there had been word from the Orange Bowl guys, but Feeley, Dunne, and Kuharich made it clear that they didn't want to be disturbed. Besides, the players were having fun. It took about a mile for them to discover that the bar car was just on the other side of the dining car. The players who were legal brought beers back for their teammates, which added to the buoyant mood of the group. Vince Tringali broke out his ukulele and had just started strumming it when Dick Colombini joined in with his accordion. Someone yelled out "Goodnight Irene," and the two moved seamlessly into the team's theme song. They took the beat from the rhythm of the steel wheels clacking over the track, and soon the players from the other car joined them, singing the song with voices that were loud and enthusiastic if not on pitch. They were on the third rendition when Burl Toler sat down beside me.

"Any word about the invitation yet?" he asked.

I told him what I had heard from Father G, adding my speculation that we would hear in a couple of days. The Orange Bowl was going to be played on New Year's Day, which was over a month away. I thought we would find out by the end of November. Toler, as usual, looked studious with his oval wire-rimmed glasses, completely at odds with the appearance he presented when he was in uniform.

"They can hardly deny us after going undefeated. Particularly with the way we won most of our games by landslides, wouldn't you think?"

"That's exactly what I think," I replied. "I just wish it was in the bag."

We listened for a moment to the raucous singing of the team song. "You know where that song, 'Goodnight Irene,' comes from?" Burl asked me.

I replied that I knew it was sung by the Weavers, a folk group, and that it had been on the Hit Parade for something like two years.

Burl nodded. "It was written by a Negro convict, Huddie Ledbetter, who was called Lead Belly. He was well known down south both as a folk singer and a hard man. He probably should have served time for any number of things, but when he was convicted and put in jail it was for something he didn't do. It was because of the testimony of a white man who was interested in the same lady that Ledbetter was courting. Lead Belly was already famous as a blues guitarist before he was locked up. He wrote that song 'Goodnight Irene' while he was in jail. It had different lyrics then, lyrics that told what he would do to the white man when he got out. The meaning was hidden in the lyrics, of course, but even so, the Weavers had to change the words. Isn't it ironic that a song of murder and revenge and social injustice toward a Negro could end up as a hit record and our theme song?"

We were just passing through Santa Barbara with glimpses of the Pacific Ocean gliding past the window. Bob St. Clair came through the door from the dining car with two beers in his hands and announced in his low voice, "They've run out of beer at the bar."

The only thing that prevented the team's passenger car from being trashed was the train porter who followed St. Clair in, announcing that the dinner buffet was now open. Everyone headed toward the dining car except Burl, who moved over to sit next to Gino sitting just across the aisle. Joe Scudero, who was next to him, was already near the front of the food line. Gino had a water glass half filled with red wine. As Burl sat down next to him, I heard him say, "Who cares if they're out of beer? They still have plenty of vino."

After the line calmed down, I joined the players going back for seconds and took my meal back to my seat in the coaches' car. There the mood was still somber.

Six hours after dinner we rolled into the station south of Market. Kuharich called a brief meeting before the team left the train. His message was simple. The president and Father Feeley had met with the Orange Bowl officials, who were impressed by our team's performance. But there was still no final acceptance. That would come from the Board of Directors of the Orange Bowl. There would be a team meeting the next day at noon in the locker room.

As the players filed out, Kuharich called the coaches and me into the rear car. Closing the doors, he gave us the full story. USF would get the invitation if we agreed to leave our two Black players at home. He was going to talk to Father Dunne the next morning. Until then, he wanted no one to talk about it. When he got mad, his eyes narrowed, his cheeks flushed, and his mouth turned down at the corners. "This does not get out until the players are told!" he said, looking at us all one by one. All the coaches knew the signs and were silent. No one would say a word. Kuharich looked directly at me and I was quick to nod my understanding.

When we had returned after the Pacific game, there had been a crowd that met us. The same had been true when we landed after the Fordham game. This time the team mood was very high, but only family members and some friends were there to greet us. It could have been the late hour, but it took the edge off the jovial mood of the entire team.

It was only after I became commissioner that I heard about the deliberations of the Orange Bowl board. The two Orange jackets flew back to Miami from Los Angeles the same day, which was why they had left in such a hurry. They met with Van Kussrow the next morning and had with them two letters. One was from the mayor of San Francisco, Elmer E. Robinson, recommending the University of San Francisco to the Orange Bowl with the full support of the city behind them; the other was more surprising. The President of the College of the Pacific and the mayor of Stockton both also encouraged the Orange Bowl board to select the Dons, an endorsement almost unprecedented in college sports. But I get ahead of myself.

Rozelle looked up and saw that the tape reel was again getting low. Kensil, who had not moved since morning, got up, stretched, and left the office for the restroom. When he came back, Rozelle said, "Good idea," and did the same. With the previous reel of tape labeled and stacked neatly on top of the first two, a fresh beer in his own hand and Kensil's, Rozelle was ready to continue the story of the '51 Dons football team.

"You know much of the story from this point on," Rozelle told Kensil. "Much of it happened in the NFL, which was strange—that the story of a college team would be continued in such dramatic fashion in the pros—but we didn't know the future at the time. I don't know that many of us slept very well that night."

Rozelle reached over and flicked a toggle switch on the recorder, stopping the reels from turning. "I'm not particularly proud of this and some of the guys are still living. This is between you and me. As I said, what happened with the Orange Bowl Board was told to me almost 17 years later at a get-together for the NFL Hall of Fame. After the meeting, we retired to the bar, and this guy from Miami started bending my ear. He was a few sheets to the wind, and someone brought up Matson, knowing I had traded for Ollie when I was with the Rams. I guess this guy wanted to look like a big man, so he started by telling everyone that for years he was on the Orange Bowl committee and in fact neither Matson nor Toler was good enough to play in that bowl game. I don't know if I was too obvious, but at least I wasn't to this guy. I bought him another drink, not that he needed it, and steered him to a booth ..."

He claimed to be on the committee in 1951 when Wood and Pratt came back from L.A. I knew he was telling the truth when he mentioned seeing the film I had sent. Van Kussrow had been in communication with Father Dunne several times during the week and had set up a projector in the board room. He started the meeting by naming the three teams that were still in the running. Most of the committee had been able to watch the two other teams as well as the Georgia Tech Yellow Jackets, in some cases more than once. Only Wood and Pratt had seen the Dons, so the first thing they did was roll the highlight reel for the rest of the board. I knew how good it was and how it made the team look. I had shot printed placards revealing the wipeout scores of each game and filmed them, inserting them into the film. As if it was needed, they drove the point home. It was quickly agreed that both the film and the record were impressive. He said that Wood even pointed out that Marchetti hadn't played in the Loyola game and it was he who had opened most of the holes Matson had used in the highlight film. He went as far as to say that the USF team was the best team he had seen that year and had a fair chance of knocking off Georgia Tech, especially if the Yellow Jackets didn't take them seriously. He went on to remind them that they had the #1 defense in the nation and were in the top five in running yardage, adding that they had the #1 running back in the nation in Matson. Publicity and interest-wise, it would be a great match-up.

Kussrow went over some of the negatives, including the small size of the University of San Francisco and the fact that they could probably expect only about 8 to 10 thousand fans to travel to Miami to attend the game. It was never a problem filling the stadium, but the city made a lot more money from visitors renting hotel rooms and going to restaurants than if the tickets were sold locally.

Pratt had stood up then and dropped the bomb. "Matson's a nigger. He's light but he's a nigger, sure as shit. So is the linebacker, Toler, number 35. He had an interception and a recovered fumble and a lot of stops in the LMU game. He was a J.C. All American and looks good in the film as well. I'm pretty sure the rest of the players are white. I got a good look at them in the locker room before the game."

The guy told me, in a slurred voice, that it had made no difference to him, but the majority of the board were incensed. No Black man had every played in a southern bowl and the Orange Bowl would certainly not be the first. It was left to Van Kussrow to tell the western school that the Black men couldn't play and that they would choose another team if their condition wasn't met. Baylor was speedily chosen as Georgia Tech's alternate opponent. It would give Tech a clear road to the National Championship. Let the pros sell themselves out by playing niggers. The Orange Bowl would remain pure, and with it their championing of southern rights and white supremacy in the game of football.

Wood, who was probably closer to Kussrow than any board member, stood up and gave his opinion. He had no problem with the choice of Baylor, but he cautioned that enough had been said about USF as a real contender for the remaining spot that it would be wise to base the board's decision purely on qualifications. He also said that he had made an unofficial inquiry while at the Dons game against Loyola. He thought the school might agree to the conditions he outlined. He also thought that if the priests did agree to the board's conditions and leave the two Black men at home, the only undefeated team west of the Mississippi would not have a chance of beating Georgia Tech.

I got to know Van Kussrow a little after I became commissioner. He was a pretty good PR man. He could spin anything. His problem was that he didn't just exaggerate the truth, as I did when I was doing P.R.; he would sell a lie. Even the way he sold the Dons' rejection showed his smarts. When asked, he let it out to the press that their schedule had just been too weak. In his opinion, the USF squad would have had four losses if they had played a representative schedule. No mention was ever made of the conditions given to Father Dunne by Pratt and relayed to Coach Kuharich on the evening after the Loyola game, while the train rattled past Pismo Beach. Dunne had relayed to Kuharich that their participation in the bowl would be favorably looked upon if they left their two Black players at home. Evidently, the president had until Monday evening to reply.

I called the waitress over and bought the guy another double, then told him I was going to the restroom and never came back. I never saw the asshole again.

CHAPTER
TWENTY-FIVE

Rozelle took a long swig of beer and turned to his friend. "You can imagine how that conversation sat with me and why I don't want it on tape. The coach was furious, barely holding his anger in check as he informed the coaches of the news just prior to the train's arrival in San Francisco. Looking directly at me, he said that what he had told us was private and was not to get out."

Rozelle swiveled his chair around, turned the recorder back on, and continued the narrative, but his voice had changed. It had a harsher edge to it. It was the tone he used when driving a point home to an owner who was defying his rules.

The players who had early classes started drifting into the locker room at 10 am, and more came at 11. I had gotten there early, but Kuharich's office door was locked, though I could hear subdued voices coming from beyond it. The locker room was filled with every player on the squad when the coach and his assistants came out, walked across the short distance from their office space, and stood before the players. The building smelled of sweat, not the sweet smell present after a hard work-out, but the sharp stink of sweat that comes from nervousness, like the way you perspire when you take a test you're not prepared for.

Kuharich entered, followed by his coaches. Until that moment I had not noticed that Ollie and Burl were not among those already in the room. After the coaches had settled in a semicircle behind Kuharich, I moved to their side. Out of the corner of my eye I saw both Ollie and Burl sneak in late and join the rest of the team. I don't think anyone at that meeting, players or coaches, would ever forget the next words Kuharich spoke.

"Men, we have received word from the Orange Bowl Committee. We will be given an invite but with a condition. Father Dunne must answer before five this afternoon." The coach stammered, as if he was having difficulty continuing his speech. "I am telling you, the team, because I feel that it is really a team decision. I also want you to know that I have already talked with both Ollie and Burl about this and I will let them speak for themselves. The Orange Bowl will give us the invite if we leave Burl and Ollie at home." Kuharich's voice got louder with each word, rushing through them as if the words burned his tongue.

At first there was a stunned silence. Then all the team voiced their outrage at once. I was standing near Bob St. Clair and remember him as the first, likely because he was the loudest and most profane. "They can shove their invite up their asses!" he yelled.

"They can't do that. We're a team!" someone else shouted.

"We all go or no one goes," said Ralph Thomas, who was standing near my right shoulder. He had not shouted, but several of his teammates heard him and echoed his refusal.

Kuharich held up his hand for quiet, but for once the Barracuda was not instantly obeyed. The team's anger kept building, everyone condemning both the restriction and the invite, as I remember it. Even those who had so much to lose, although most of them hadn't thought their way through it yet, were shouting at the top of their lungs. Even the normally quiet Marchetti issued a "Screw them!"

Eventually Kuharich's plea for quiet was noticed and the noise was replaced with angry stares and heavy breathing, the players who were seated now on the edge of their benches, those who were still standing placing one leg in front of the other in a fighter's stance.

"This is nothing new. There has never been a Negro player allowed to participate in any of the southern bowls."

"Tell those candy-ass rednecks to shove it. Burl and Ollie go or no one goes!" yelled St. Clair, evoking another round of protests, which Kuharich quelled by raising both hands in the air.

"I have already spoken with Burl and Ollie. I would like you to listen to them before you give me your answer. Also, keep in mind that this is, finally, a university decision. It will be Father Dunne who will ultimately answer for the team and there is a lot that goes into this besides whether Burl and Ollie play. Burl." Kuharich motioned Toler up to the front of the room. The coach continued to stand next to him.

The room was quiet, everyone anticipating what Burl had to say. His voice was low, almost gentle, and he looked like the scholar that he was. "Ollie and I found out about this this morning. We knew that this was a possibility as soon as the bowl was mentioned. I come from Tennessee, Ollie from Texas. We have experienced firsthand the culture that spawned this decision. Both Ollie and I think the team has won the honor with its play. Neither of us wants you to give up what has been a fantastic season on our account. We advise you to take the offer. We understand and will support your decision."

Without coordinating their actions, spontaneously, Ed Brown at 6'2" and Joe Scudero at 5'8" walked to the front of the room to stand with Ollie and Burl. Brown spoke first. "Burl, you and Ollie are team players. There is not a player in this room who would expect you to say anything other than what you have just said. But the Geek is right. This is a team, a whole team, and we don't give up on teammates. The team goes or no one goes."

Scudero, in his south of Market accent, added, addressing Matson, "I just watched you have the greatest season in history. Coach asked me to understand that my yards would suffer so that you could make All-American. I did that because it was good for the team. If we go without you, it won't be good for the team. It won't be good for any of us individually, either. Everyone in this room would regret it for the rest of their lives."

The room exploded with affirmative shouts of support.

Brown, the senior quarterback, turned to Kuharich. "I guess you have your answer, Coach. It's not a no, but a *hell* no!"

Kuharich watched as the players crowded around Ollie and Burl, shaking their hands, expressing their support. Kuharich had his answer. As he turned to leave, I saw a tear run down his cheek. I got up and followed the coaches out of the locker room.

Kuharich slammed the door to his office once we were all inside. I didn't know if I was invited, but I wasn't asked to leave.

"Damn. I'll never have another team like this one. I'd give my arm to coach them in that game. We'd win, too. When I heard the news on the train coming back, Dunne said it was up to me and he would support me in whatever I decided. Heck of a thing, to pass the buck to me like that, but I guess that's what I just did with the team. Last night I thought I would just tell the team that we wouldn't accept the terms. Then I talked with Matson and Toler this morning. They were a lot calmer than I was. They asked to speak to the team first. They wanted me to accept the conditions. I thought it was the wrong thing to do, but then I started thinking about how I'd coach against the Yellow Jackets without them. I mean, we got by without Gino at Loyola. Given what just happened, I'm sorry I even gave it a thought. I'm proud of the team. Now I have to get our answer to the president. I think he will honor the team's decision, but I understand that doing so will cost the university the program and the school a lot of money."

In the president's office, looking out on the green grass common fronting Fulton Street, Father Dunne paced with his hands behind his back. He watched Coach Kuharich exit the building and walk toward the athletic facility to the south. Feeley sat in a chair in front of the large desk and swiveled to follow the man's movements. It was one-thirty in the afternoon and Kuharich had just left. Feeley told me about their conversation later.

"I wish Kuharich had not given the players a voice in the decision," said Dunne. "It would have been much better if he had made the decision."

"Would it have made a difference?" asked Feeley. "I mean that the team would likely still have responded the same way. Besides, everything in our creed tells us to respect the vulnerable, the disadvantaged, the underprivileged."

"I understand that, but I am also the president of this university and my priority is keeping it open and functioning. With our enrollment shrinking, my ability to do so is in question. This opportunity not only involves a significant amount of money but would give us national recognition and surely an increase in the number of applications."

"Our first obligation is to do what is morally right. No one is a bigger supporter of this team than I am. You know that," said Feeley, rising to his feet, his voice soft and reasonable, knowing that Dunne was beset with the problems of running an institution of which the football program was only a part. "If you reflect, the team's decision made it easier for you to make the decision, not harder. I know that in your heart, you could never condone the bigotry of the Orange Bowl in presenting you with this dilemma."

Father Dunne turned away from the window, a smile growing on his face, the frown wrinkles on his brow smoothing over.

"You're absolutely right. But this is not a dilemma. That is being caught on the horns without having a correct solution. This problem has a solution." Moving to his desk, he consulted a notepad on his desk on which he had written the phone number of Van Kussrow. He picked up the phone and began dialing.

The city's papers were filled with the news of Baylor's selection. The Bears had lost three games and were the runner-up in the southwest conference. Georgia Tech was unbeaten but had a tie on their record. USF vs. Georgia Tech would have been a natural pairing. As it was, Tech needed a last-minute field goal to win 17 to 14 over Baylor.

The Orange Bowl caught heat not only from the west coast press but also from the national publications. Some of the reasons that were leaked by the Orange Bowl Board for USF's exclusion were what you might expect—for instance, that USF's schedule had been third-rate. But the comment I remember to this day was one that came out of the *Miami Herald* in support of the decision: "No one would remember the players from this tiny private west coast school." More than any other rationalization they spewed as to why the Dons were left out in the cold, that statement ended up proving their dishonesty and wrongheadedness.

What mildly surprised me then and has come to amaze me more and more since I have become an administrator was the university's decision. Here was a university that had been around forever, since 1855 or something. This was their first football team that had achieved national prominence. They had declining enrollment due to the Korean War draft. They were in serious financial difficulty. They would have made upwards of $75,000 in the bowl, but just as important, they would have put their school on the map; applications would likely have doubled. That always happens when a school wins a national championship in football or basketball. It was ultimately not the team's decision, nor

Kuharich's; it was Father Dunne's. I have no doubt the president could have insisted that the team play. I know Kuharich would have done so had the team not reacted as they had, and both Matson and Toler would have urged their teammates to comply.

But Father Dunne didn't do that. He supported the team's collective decision on moral grounds. He was a brilliant man. I have no doubt he knew the hardship his decision would cause the university as well as many of the players. The next year there was no football program at USF, but Father Dunne continued the scholarships for the players who hadn't graduated. The NCAA had not made that a rule in '51. It is one of the reasons I still support USF whenever I can.

The point was cemented for me the next day when I heard an exchange between Burl Toler and Gino Marchetti. Toler had already been drafted by Cleveland's NFL team. I had just informed him that he was selected to play for the senior All-Stars against the NFL Champions. If I had known that Burl would hurt his knee so badly he would never play a down in the NFL, I wouldn't have been so excited about delivering the news. It was one of the reasons that I abolished the game in 1976. I should have done it sooner, but there was a lot I had to get fixed those first few years I was commissioner and the owners liked the game for whatever reason.

Gino came over, his head down, looking like someone had stolen his Harley-Davidson. I shook hands with Burl and stayed close as the two friends shook hands.

"This is bullshit," said Marchetti as he took his friend's hand, waving a newspaper in the other. "You're the best player on the team. You and Ollie are getting hosed."

"You got it all wrong, Gino. Ollie and I are used to it. You saw what those southerners who played for Camp Pendleton and the San Diego Navy were like. Ollie and I can take care of it on the field, but in the boardroom, in the courts, with the police, we can't. Our color defines what sort of treatment we get. Not here in San Francisco as much, but in a lot of the rest of the country. Ollie's father was not even allowed to vote before they came here. It's really you and the rest of the guys who are getting the dirty end of the stick."

"It still stinks. Something should be done to those guys."

"What they did is perfectly legal. The laws let them do it, so they do."

"Yeah, but..."

"Gino, let me tell you story about a woman with courage. It concerns a Negro businesswoman named Viola Desmond. Last year in Oklahoma, you saw the Colored Only bathrooms and the segregated hotel we had to stay in during that trip. Well, the same things happen in Canada, which is odd because Canada was the final destination for the Drinking Gourd—the Freedom Train escape route from the south during the Civil War. This woman, Viola Desmond, lived in Nova Scotia. She went to a movie, but she didn't know it was a segregated theater. After sitting down, she was told she would have to move to the rear of the upstairs balcony. She refused and was arrested—went to trial and was convicted—on the charge of failure to pay the one-cent entertainment tax for that seat in the whites-only section. She fought the conviction, showing it for what it was. She has suffered both in business and in society the last five years, but she keeps the injustice in the forefront of the minds of Canadians by continued attempts to overturn her conviction.

"This is the same type of thing, but since the Orange Bowl is a private organization, it is not a fight we can win. But mark my words, Gino. Sooner or later some Black person here will challenge the laws that allow this to happen. It might even be a woman like Viola Desmond, but it will happen."

Of course, it did happen, thirteen years later in 1964 with Martin Luther King's voting rights marches in Selma and the passing of the Civil Rights Act and the Voting Rights Act. Even before that, remember the young Black girl Elizabeth Eckford who entered an all-white school in Little Rock in 1957. She was supposed to meet eight other Black students to enter the school together, but the meeting place was changed the night before and Eckford's family did not have a phone. So she ended up entering the school alone, while the others were snuck in through the back door. An angry mob forced her to go home, but a few weeks later, she and the other eight students entered the school again together. It was far from the end of the struggle, but it was a beginning. So Burl was right.

A Black man eventually played in a southern bowl game in 1956. He had a Dutch name and played for a team from the northeast. The invite was issued and accepted. No one realized that he was Black until he was seen practicing a few days prior to the game. A newspaper reporter finally saw him on the practice field and wrote an article. There was a storm of letters and talk of cancelling the game, but strong threats from the federal government, as well as fear of law suits from the vendors, forced the game forward. The man played, as the team said it would withdraw at the last minute if he was denied. So it finally happened—by mistake—five years after Ollie and Burl were turned away from the Orange Bowl and the USF Dons were prevented from playing for a national title.

CHAPTER TWENTY-SIX

Ten of the seniors on the USF squad were drafted by the NFL that year, with a total of eleven if you count Bob St. Clair. St. Clair was only a junior and was drafted the next year after he was forced to transfer to Tulsa to play football while he earned his degree. Ten were drafted out of a total of 17 seniors; eight finished by playing in the league. There were only 38 players on the squad, unlike at some of the bigger schools with a hundred players as we see today. Matson, Marchetti, and St. Clair were cinches to make the NFL Hall of Fame, and possibly Dick Stanfel from the 1950 team as well. There were six players from that '51 team who played in the same Pro Bowl game in 1956. Little Joe Scudero was on that roster. Six players from the same college squad! Can you believe it? It will probably never happen again. Ed Brown played quarterback for the Chicago Bears for 14 years. He entered the Marine Corps directly after graduation and joined the Bears in 1954. He was the first Bear to lead the NFL in passing in 1956. He was never surrounded by a good team, but his arm was always considered one of the best in the NFL and he was always a threat to run. He still made the Pro Bowl twice.

Burl Toler was special. I mentioned how he tore up his knee in the American Football Classic. He went back to USF and got a master's degree. He started teaching right there in San Francisco at a junior high school about a half-mile from the campus. It took a while for his knee to heal, but after it did he started to officiate high school and college games. I made him the first Black official in the NFL. He was a good one. He worked Super Bowls on merit. More than that, he has become a great friend.

Bob St. Clair likes to tell this story about Burl. It was Burl's first year officiating. He was standing on the sidelines and St. Clair came up behind Burl and grabbed him from behind, lifting him off the ground. Burl is a big man and very strong. Not many people could have done that. He struggled and broke St. Clair's hold. Bob said he kept saying, "Burl, it's me, Saint!" I was watching from Vince Morabito's box. Burl actually ran about ten yards down the sideline before he turned and shouted back at St. Clair to stop.

I might have been the luckiest one. I parlayed that season into getting a job with the L.A. Rams. It was a perfect opportunity and a good example of being in the right place at the right time. Eleven years later I was the general manager, and after that, commissioner.

You know how I just said luck is being in the right place at the right time? I grew up in Compton, actually Lynwood, which is right next door and too small to have a high school. Compton is just a little south of L.A., a few miles inland from the L.A. airport and Manhattan Beach. I played basketball but was kind of a runt. My parents were so worried about my size that they pulled me out of school for a year and sent me to work on a relative's farm in Modesto. That's way up north in the Central Valley. I was never really buff, but I was a lot more physically mature after those ten months. Our family, like most others then, was often short on money. Most of the kids in high school had part-time jobs. I was lucky; I got on part-time with the Long Beach *Press-Telegram*. The hours were great, as most of the work at the newspaper was done in the afternoon after school got out. That's where I got my start in journalism and learned how the press worked.

My dad had been in the navy in World War I, and after high school, all my friends started enlisting, most of them in the navy, so I tried. As I mentioned earlier, it didn't go so well. I was initially rejected for being colorblind, but through some twists of fate and fortune, I eventually found my way into the navy. I was put on an old converted tanker named the Gardoqui. Held a crew of 70, and our job was to sail in small circles in the Pacific and fuel ships that came to us. It was 1944, and when the war ended, we were sent to Japan for a few months, then back home by way of the Panama Canal to Mobile, where I was discharged.

"Didn't you tell me that you ran a football pool on the ship?" asked Kensil.

"Yep, I did. It was the war, but our duty was so monotonous that the crew would do anything for a little excitement, and it made me a few bucks."

"Did you ever run a book?"

"Not really, but I did make one bet that won me a pile. The crew was filled with mid-west types. It seemed that the further away from saltwater a kid grew up, the more likely it was that he had joined the navy. Almost all of them were Notre Dame fans. That year the Irish were playing Army. Army was loaded. I think I knew more about football than anyone else on board, but it might have been that they were so biased that they were going to bet on Notre Dame no matter what. I gave them the Irish and eight points. Army won 49 to zip."

"Should I tell Mr. Davis about that?"

"Don't even kid about that. Besides, it wasn't gambling. There was no way in the world that Army doesn't win that game."

Back to being in the right place at the right time. I took advantage of the G. I. Bill, went back to Compton, and entered junior college. Along with a friend of mine, Myron De Long, who had also been in the navy, I set up the Compton News Bureau. It primarily covered the junior college football team, which was pretty darn good at the time, but we expanded into other sports as well. It made us a little money, and with tuition being paid, we thought we were in hog heaven. My ambition at that time was to be the sports editor of the *Los Angeles Times*.

So, what happens? The Cleveland Rams, who had just won the championship, moved to Los Angeles and got a great lease at the L.A. Coliseum. They couldn't practice there, so they rented Compton's J.C. facilities. The Rams moved their pre-season training camp right to me. They had hired a local for their publicity director, a fellow named Maxwell Stiles. I'd gotten to know him a little when I was in high school and working for the *Press-Telegram*. I guess he liked me. Either that or he was just lazy and didn't want to drive to L.A., but he came into the small office we had and gave us the job of putting together the programs for the Rams' pre-season games. For us, a couple of kids just out of the service and two years out of high school, it was like being at Disneyland.

When the Rams moved to Los Angeles for the regular season, we went back to covering the J. C. football team and any other athletic events of interest. That was why we attended a college basketball game in which USF was playing USC—that and the fact that I had talked my way into free tickets for being a member of the press. Pete Newell was the Dons' coach and we asked for an interview. Pete was a very intelligent man, full of curiosity. He gave us a nice interview, but he asked us as many questions as we asked him. I might have exaggerated a little about the publicity we had done for the Rams. He told us that if we wanted to get a university degree, we should come to USF, and that he could use some help with publicity. That's how I ended up at USF.

School had always been easy for me. I hardly ever studied, just crammed for exams. I still had the G.I. Bill, and I wanted a four-year degree. Newell set up an interview for me with Charles Harney, the same booster I mentioned earlier who was with the president at the Loyola game. He gave me a job that was basically a money supplement for what I was doing for the basketball team and the next year for Kuharich. Very quickly I saw that the USF job had real potential for advancing what I then thought would be my career in the fourth estate.

Soon after De Long and I arrived in San Francisco, the men's soccer team won the National Championship, and no one knew anything about it. Newell and Kuharich were great recruiters and fantastic coaches. It was my job to let everyone know about their programs. I decided to get my feet wet by helping the soccer team, whose season started in the beginning of summer. It would help me get acquainted with the local papers and learn to find my way around USF.

De Long had heard about this soccer player who was supposed to be a prince. I never really checked out the truth of that, but he was colorful enough. He would walk around campus in his tribal gowns. We took pictures of him on the field with his tribal get-up on, kicking a ball, and bombarded the local papers with press releases. Coach Negoesco was astounded by the interest that one story drew, and so was the school—so much so that they rented Kezar for the next match against Temple. The largest crowd they had attracted the previous year had been five hundred fans. They pulled ten thousand to watch a prince play soccer against Temple. That was the clincher. I now fully understood how the press could help promote a team if they were given the right help with a compelling story.

But you wanted to know how I got the NFL Commissioner's job. Well, the story is kind of convoluted. The USF program had been ditched after the '51 season. Matson was picked number one in the NFL draft, Kuharich took an NFL head coaching position. Even the basketball program changed. Pete Newell went to Cal, where he won a national title, giving his job to Phil Woolpert, a good guy I used to play cards with twice a week. I didn't realize how good a coach he had become under Newell, but two years later he had Bill Russell, K. C. Jones, and Mike Farmer, and the rest is history. They won the NIA their sophomore year, which was then considered the national title, then the NCAA the next two years. Three championships in three years.

At the time, though, in 1952, I saw no future in staying at USF. Charlie Harney, the developer, offered me a full-time job, but I was still not finished with the toy department of sports. The Rams were having their pre-season practices at the University of Redlands. I dropped over to say hello the day after Tex Maule, who had been their director of publicity, quit. Tex Schramm, the GM, remembered me from when we did the first pre-season programs for him and hired me on the spot. He had been watching the Dons' season in preparation for the NFL draft and noticed the publicity I had engendered for the team. He laughed when he told me he hadn't believed my exaggerated pre-game hype but later thought I had undersold the team when he saw the results. I thought, "Great, another Rosenthal."

Dan Reeves was the Rams' owner, and a more organized man I have never met. Everything we did had a system. He hired great people and expected them to be creative and do their jobs. His organization became the standard for the NFL as people left and took with them the forms and protocols developed by Reeves to use with their new teams. I stayed with the Rams for two years doing publicity; then Ken Macker, who ran an advertising agency in San Francisco, offered me a job for twice the money. Ken had just taken over the contract for Pan Am Airlines, which was one of the main sponsors of the 1956 Olympics in Australia. He needed help and gave me that contract to work. I came up with the idea of using the koala bear as a symbol. It was a success and is still used today by the Australian tourist bureau.

During that time, I married Jane, whom I had first met while I was in the navy. At 26 years old, I guess I felt I should act like an adult. Maybe I started to look like one as well, because two years after I had started with Ken, the Rams called about the general manager's job. Tex Schramm had left to take a position in the growing television industry, and Tex and Bert Bell, then the Commissioner of the NFL, recommended me to Dan Reeves. I liked Dan and I guess he liked me. All of a sudden, at 26 years old, I was in charge of one of the NFL's most valuable products. I signed a contract for four years at $25,000 per year.

Three years later Bert Bell died of a heart attack. The owners met in Miami to discuss picking the next commissioner. The owners were all rich, powerful men used to getting their own way. Everyone wanted to protect their own team first and the league second. I won't go into detail, but they went twenty-three ballots trying to agree on a new man. There were three men who were pivotal to the selection: George Halas, George Preston Marshall, and Carroll Rosenbloom. Finally, Paul Brown of the Browns had had enough. He could see that the four men who had been put up already were on a merry-go-round and would remain so unless the owners were offered an alternative. He politicked in secret, letting each of the powers think that they would be the power behind my nomination. So, at 33 years of age, on the twenty-fourth ballot, I became the Commissioner of the NFL. I had won the vote eight to one with my owner, Dan Reeves, by necessity abstaining. Oddly enough, the only vote cast against me was San Francisco. The first thing I did was move the NFL offices from Philadelphia to New York. The night of the vote, Dan Reeves came to me in my room, and I told him about the move. He warned me that New York was a different beast, and I had best wear a coat and hat at all times there. My experience and success with Grantland Rice and the other sports writers nine years ago told me otherwise. Dan insisted that I buy a hat! I did. It's on the hanger in the reception area. I've never worn it.

CHAPTER
TWENTY-SEVEN

After the '51 season, the team disbanded. I mentioned that ten players were drafted and Ollie was selected in the first round of the draft, the third overall pick of the Chicago Cardinals. If proof was needed that racism was alive and well in 1951, you only had to know that after leading the nation in rushing yards and starring as starting running back in the East-West Shrine Game, Ollie made Grantland Rice's All-American team as a defensive back.

Merrill Peacock joined Ollie with the Chicago Cardinals. The Cardinals must have liked what they saw scouting the Dons because they also drafted Mike Mergen and Roy Barni. Red Stephens and Ralph Thomas were also drafted by the Cardinals but entered the armed services instead, where they played on the football team for the next two years. Thomas joined the Washington Redskins in 1955. After his stint in the Marine Corps, Ed Brown went to the Chicago Bears, where he continued his good play and his late-night partying for the next eleven years. Dick Stanfel went to the Detroit Lions, where he helped them to a championship in 1953. But others were not as fortunate. I mentioned that St. Clair had to transfer to Tulsa for his senior year to play football so he wouldn't fall off the NFL's recruiting map. Joe Scudero stayed but took mostly acting classes his final year. Without football, he fell off the scouts' radar and after graduation joined the Toronto Argonauts of the Canadian Football League. After earning All-League status his first year, he was offered a spot on the Washington Redskins, where he was reunited with Ralph Thomas. Little Joe was selected for the Pro Bowl in 1956 along with five of his Dons teammates. He also talked his way into five movies, mostly westerns, fulfilling his acting desires. In his adulthood, this most undiplomatic of Dons became a diplomat serving overseas in the Ambassador Corps for both Democratic and Republican administrations.

Dick Colombini, Dick Huxley, and several others joined the ROTC, ensuring that they would follow Vince Tringali in fighting for our country in Korea. Hal Sachs went back to the beaches of San Diego, where he started a cleaning business that became quite successful. In fact, almost the entire team was successful in one form or another. Bill Henneberry, the second-string quarterback and in many ways the glue of the team, joined the USF staff and continued to work in Development while keeping the team connected with five-year reunions as the individuals moved on to their own endeavors. I tried never to miss a reunion. It was such a great group. The players knew they had been part of something special, and as time went on, their stand became recognized and then the stuff of legend. I was accepted as a part of it and was as proud as they were.

Ollie had been a track star before he turned to football. With the summer Olympics coming up later that year, he petitioned the U. S. Olympic Committee to allow him to try out for the team in the 400-meter dash. He was initially denied by Avery Brundage. However, Brundage, who was the head of the U. S. Olympic Committee, was about to be given an upgrade, becoming president of the International Olympic Committee. Ollie's ruling was modified when Brundage, long suspected of being a racist, left for his new job. That allowed Ollie to qualify if he could attain a certain time standard in the 400 before the qualifying meet. The committee said they didn't think it was possible for a football player to lose the weight and gain the straight-ahead speed of a world-class track athlete in just two months. It didn't surprise me a bit that his teammates joined Ollie in taking up the challenge.

The trials were in late spring, but by the time Ollie got his invite, he had little more than a month for training. His hamstring was still tight and he wanted to lose fifteen pounds. At first he worked out by himself, getting the keys to Kezar and running laps and intervals. Then he moved to the east coast to train for a month at Triborough. Triborough Stadium had been the site of the Fordham game. Its open end looked across the water directly at the Manhattan skyline. It also had a great running track around the football field, a surface that was the exact makeup of the Olympic trial venue. I never found out if it had been Ollie who called out for help because his times were not dropping fast enough, or whether Burl and Scooter decided on their own to help him. But to no one's surprise, Burl Toler and Joe Scudero went with Ollie to the east coast.

By the time they arrived at Triborough, Ollie had already lost ten pounds. He wasn't fat to begin with and the weight loss made him look chiseled, but he still hadn't approached the needed qualifying time. The three of them set up a two-a-day schedule based on Kuharich's Camp Corning, except they used water in their training. Each session was two hours long, with the first half-hour of each session devoted solely to stretching. A lot of the stretches required Burl to physically push the muscles in Ollie's legs slowly past the point of resistance that his teammate could not endure on his own. Scudero did not have the strength or the height to perform the duty as well as Burl could, being Ollie's equal in size and strength. Scooter made up for it by working Ollie's core strength between Burl's stretches. Half an hour was spent on starts, with either Burl or Scudero lining up with Ollie and calling the count, guaranteeing they would get the break and be in front of Ollie for the first five steps. When Scudero took off, being quicker, he was able to maintain a lead for almost 100 meters. They would then run a set of four 400-meter intervals with a two-minute rest in between, trying to lower the time for each of the four. The problem was that neither of them could stay with Ollie for the entire distance.

Ollie had spent some of his signing bonus on a foldable massage table, and his two friends spent another hour after each workout rubbing him down, trying to lengthen the muscles of his legs and butt. The times dropped but were still two-tenths of a second above the set standard. Then Burl had an idea. He told Scooter about it and they both chuckled.

The next 400 meters, Scooter lined up on Ollie's inside and when both were ready, sent them off the blocks. The 400 is a grueling race. It is not a sprint, because you have to breathe, and there is no way you can run full out for the entire distance. Yet it is too short for strategy to play a major role, as it does in the half-mile or the mile, where you have several times around the track to get in position, draft on other runners, and time your sprint. It does not rely heavily on the start, as does the 100-meter dash, which can be won or lost on the blocks. The 200 can be run almost at full speed by a trained athlete but is not as conditional on the blocks. The 400 relies on strength, speed, and guts.

When Scudero started the race, he took at least a step down the track before he shouted "Go!" Ollie had no idea what was about to happen. As usual, Scudero was quicker out of the blocks and passed through the hundred slightly ahead as well, but instead of lengthening his stride and creating a pace that would allow him to still be standing at the end, the little man kept up his speed and led Ollie by a foot through the 200 mark. Ollie was working hard to keep up with Scooter, who was running full out, but he knew he would pass him in the second half of the race. Then he saw Burl standing on the track in Scudero's lane as if waiting for a baton hand-off. There was none, but there was a hand slap, and Toler, who was already in full stride, took off for the second half of the distance. Burl wasn't a world-class track athlete, but he wasn't slow either. He pulled away from Matson for the next 100 yards.

Ollie Matson was so soft-spoken and quiet that most people didn't realize how competitive he was or how much he hated to lose. Anyone watching the Camp Pendleton or the San Diego Navy Training Depot teams would have seen flashes of this quality, but he usually kept it well hidden. Now with his friend threatening to beat him in the last part of the race, he pushed himself to close the distance. Slowly he drew on Toler, but he was still a yard behind him as they passed the finish line.

Scudero was standing at the finish line, a stopwatch in his hand, still winded from his effort in the first 200 meters of the race.

"Well, you got your qualifying mark by two tenths," he said to Matson, who was still bent over, his hands on his knees. Toler looked up from his similar position, a wide smile on his face. "We figured you just needed a bit of competition to get your juices flowing," added Scudero, the only one of the three who had breath to speak.

Over the next two weeks, all three men became fitter and faster. Ollie's starts improved as well. At the end of their stay, no matter how they tried, no matter how much of a jump Scudero took off the line at the start, Burl and Joe couldn't beat Ollie to the finish line.

Ollie was off to the Olympics. He took an individual bronze medal in the 400-meter race and a silver in the 1600-meter relay race. Going to the Cardinals right after the Olympics, Ollie became rookie of the year in the NFL. Then, believing he should serve his country, he entered the army, returning to the Cardinals after a year in 1954.

That year, 1951, when the Dons should have played for the national title, if you asked Ollie about the discrimination he endured, he would always talk about the first Tulsa game, in which the Oklahoma team had asked Kuharich not to bring any Black players. It's significant that he would remember that, not the 1566 yards of run yardage or the 21 touchdowns or being awarded All-American status that year not as a runner but as a defensive back. He also did not mention the two black eyes and bruises he suffered without getting a call for being hit after the whistle or the three touchdowns he scored that were all called back by the southern officials. In retrospect, it was a precursor to the bowl decision.

When I asked Ollie if he ever considered himself a forerunner of Black players in the NFL, he shook his head and said that that honor went to Fritz Pollard and Paul Robeson. Pollard was the first to play in a bowl game, the Rose Bowl in 1916, and Robeson turned professional to pay for his law school tuition at Columbia. In modern times, Kenny Washington and Woody Strode had made big news five years before by turning professional out of UCLA, and Jackie Robinson did so in professional baseball in 1947. I persisted and told Ollie that many considered him a hero. He just laughed and said that that title rightly belonged to Rosa Parks, who in 1955, just a few years after he graduated from USF, had been arrested in Montgomery, Alabama for refusing to give up her seat on a bus to a white man.

I kind of worry about Ollie. I try to phone him every couple of weeks and see him when I'm on the west coast, but he seems distant, and last time I had to tell him who I was.

Of all the players on the team, Gino Marchetti probably surprised me the most. He also played in the East-West Shrine game. He was drafted in the second round by the New York Yanks and without leaving their roster, he managed to play for three teams the first year. The Yanks became the Dallas Texans and then the

Baltimore Colts in 1953. It emphasized how unstable the league was in those formative years. It wasn't a surprise that Gino became a great player. He played for 13 years, won two world championships, was nine times All-Pro, and played in 11 Pro bowls. He was voted the greatest defensive end in football history in 1972. All of that didn't surprise me, but that he became a very successful businessman did. Right in the middle of his great years in Baltimore, Gino decided to open a string of restaurants called Gino's.

Marchetti, like most players in those years, had to work other jobs during off season. Gino would go back to the west coast and work in the sheriff's department in Contra Costa County, or at the iron mill at Sparrow Point near Antioch, where he would lug steel around the yard. Then, after the shifts were over, he would bartend at his older brother Lino's bar.

After the 1958 championship game, in which Gino was awarded the game ball for stopping Frank Gifford, at the same time breaking two bones in his ankle, Carroll Rosenbloom suggested that he take advantage of his fame and do something in business in Baltimore. I always respected Carroll for his business sense, and particularly for taking care of his players, especially Gino. Gino's teammate, Alan Ameche, had already started a string of high-end hamburger places. Gino had noticed a chain on the west coast by the name of McDonald's and thought a lower-priced hamburger would be better without competing with Ameche's restaurants.

Rosenbloom staked him $100,000 to open the first Gino's. Knowing Carroll, he got a good return on his investment. In the first year, the place was making $15,000 a month. Nine years later there were 65 Gino's restaurants, and in 1982 there were 313. Gino was making more money than I was. They sold the chain for $48 million to Marriott, with Gino getting a big chunk of it. Marriott made most of them into Roy Rogers restaurants and the rest into Kentucky Fried Chickens. If you asked Gino, he would simply say that he was "a big dumb guy who was just standing there, saying yes."

Of all the players on that team, and with all the success they have had both in the NFL and in business, I think the most all-around successful individual is one who never played football in the NFL. Burl Toler, as I have explained, was drafted in his junior year by the Cleveland team but ruined his knee in the College All-Stars vs. the Pro Champions game after graduation. He had surgery but would never play football again. Instead, he went back to USF and earned his teaching degree. As he recovered his ability to run, he worked high school and college games as an official and in 1965 applied to the NFL. As he was fond of pointing out, "There was no mention of race during the process." He applied, he was qualified, he passed the tests, and he became an official. He was quiet about the fact that he was the first African-American official in any of the major sports. Baseball would follow three years later, and the National Basketball Association ten years after Burl took the step, but he never considered himself a pioneer. He ignored the insults from the stands and the language from the players and just did his job.

Burl thought the advancement of his race in America had to be accomplished through education before demonstrations. He counseled his students to follow their own agendas through learning and not to listen to the "shouters." He taught and later became principal of Portola Junior High School, the first African-American school administrator in San Francisco. He was a true inspiration to all who knew him.

AFTERWORD

The genesis of this book came about toward the end of my service as the interim Athletic Director at the University of San Francisco. A producer from Hollywood visited me at my office. He laid out plans to create a movie about the '51 Dons football team. There was something about the individual that I didn't care for. I asked him what the message of the story would be in his film. He answered quickly that it was the terrible discrimination two African-American players on the team had experienced. I thanked him and told him we would consider his proposal. A movie hopefully would be made; however, the message would not be that Burl Toler and Ollie Matson had had to endure discrimination. They had, of course, but in those years, so had almost every Black American. The real story, to my way of thinking, was that thirty-five of their teammates and their university had joined them in standing up to that discrimination.

Years later I talked with Bill Henneberry and his wife Jeanie in their house in San Bruno, some thirty minutes south of the University of San Francisco. I found myself reflecting on the route I was driving and the great changes and improvements in traveling that have been seen in the last hundred years. My grandmother and grandfather had been married on April 16th, two days before the great San Francisco earthquake of 1906. They had traveled this route past the future Henneberry home to Santa Cruz, a two-flat-tire trip in their car over mostly dirt roads. They cut their honeymoon short to return to the devastation that was San Francisco. Twelve years later, my mother was born in Palo Alto because they could not reliably get back to the city and the hospital in time for the delivery. In 1951, the year of this story, there were few freeways and not enough traffic to necessitate them. Things had certainly changed. In recounting the story of the team, it would be important to remember those changes, both physical and cultural, that had occurred in the years since 1951.

I had met Bill Henneberry, a remarkable man, some twelve years before when I first joined the Athletic Department of the University of San Francisco. Bill had asked me if I would like to play golf with him and a friend of his, Sam Johnstone. Sam had been a three-sport man at USF, lettering in football, basketball, and track years before, and he had started a foundation to help support the USF golf teams.

I was amazed by Sam's vitality. He was eighty-seven years old and he practically ran from shot to shot, easily shooting his age that day. He had flown bombers in World War II and had come home to start an aeronautical supply and parts business, specializing in vintage and wartime aircrafts. Two remarkable things happened during that round. Somewhere around the sixth hole I discovered that Sam had grown up half a block from my mother's home on Dewey Boulevard. Hers was the very house we had moved back into in 1951. Sam and my mother were the same age and had been best friends. The other important development was that I became friends with Bill Henneberry.

When I first came to USF, I knew about the '51 football team on some level. In those years, you could not grow up in San Francisco without gaining a visceral understanding of that team and that season. However, I was unaware then of how instrumental Henneberry had been that year as the backup quarterback, and of the role he had played for the team and university in the years since, organizing reunions and serving as the hub of connection between the university and the team. Through Bill, I learned the true story of the football team that went undefeated yet refused to play in a National Title game on a collective moral principle. Sometime during that afternoon I spent with Bill and Jeanie, I decided to write the history of the individuals who had come together that year. The book would not necessarily focus on the facts or scores, or even on the players' stand against segregation; that had been thoroughly covered in newspaper articles, television documentaries, and a book by Kristine Setting Clark. Instead I felt compelled to write the story of these remarkable young men and their upbringings, which had forged their ability to take their stand and perform these deeds of valor, and of the university that had brought them together and helped to shape their moral compass.

ACKNOWLEDGEMENTS

Any author is indebted to many individuals who help them with a novel. This is especially true when the work is about a true event. I am no different.

First and foremost, my recognition and thanks to the '51 Dons who lived the story. Bob St. Clair, Gino Marchetti, Ralph Thomas, Dick Colombini, Joe Scudero, Bill Henneberry, and Father John Lo Schiavo sat for numerous filmed interviews, allowing me not only to understand the events firsthand but also to appreciate the style, personalities, backgrounds, and morals of each of these men.

Thanks to Art Ciocca, Lynn McShane, and Richard Petrocchi, who from the very beginning said that this story had to be told.

Thanks also to Charlie Cross, a friend and Vice President of the University of San Francisco, who granted me the time and space to write this novel and supported me in my endeavors as a coach and athletic director. Without Charlie, this novel wouldn't have been written.

A special thanks to Father Paul Fitzgerald, whose compassion and understanding helped me over a rough spot. I will always be grateful.

Thanks to Julie Congi if for nothing else than her smile and her infectious laughter, and also for leading the remaining group of players to the Fiesta Bowl, for which she was awarded a signed football. I suspect that every institution has someone like Julie, who knows everyone and everything and is loved by all.

Thanks to the USF library staff, particularly Matthew Collins, who helped me locate yearbooks, game programs, and background material and gave me access to the archives of the San Francisco newspapers that followed the triumphs of this team.

Thanks to Kristine Clark for writing *Undefeated, Untied, and Uninvited* and *St. Clair: I'll Take It Raw!* and relating many aspects of that season.

Special thanks to Sarah Goss, the self-confessed word junkie who not only reads my works and edits them but straightens me out on details large and small.

Lest we forget, thanks to the board of the 1951 Orange Bowl for their insistence that Burl and Ollie stay home. Few people remember who won the Orange Bowl that year, while the '51 Dons have become legend.

Finally, the ultimate thanks to my wife Kellie, who puts up with all my quirks.

Gary Nelson lives in Marin County, California with his wife, Kellie, and their two Springer spaniels, and close to his four semi-launched children. He can be found driving the back roads of Marin most summer days in his 1957 TR-3.

This is a fictionalized account of an amazing true story. Most of the details and dialogue were captured from extensive interviews, both oral and filmed, with various surviving members of the '51 Dons, particularly Bob St. Clair, Gino Marchetti, Joe Scudero, Fr. John Lo Schiavo, Dick Colombini, and Ralph Thomas. Still, there were some events that must have happened and conversations that must have taken place that I have had to construct from my imagination. Those that Rozelle had with the coaches and those concerning the Orange Bowl selection come particularly to mind. For those I tried to be as faithful to the story as a work of fiction can be, often relying on newspaper accounts of the day.

Gary Nelson

CPSIA information can be obtained
at www.ICGtesting.com
Printed in the USA
FSHW011312150819
61085FS